PATHS LESS TRAVELED

by

Dennis Aprill

PATHS LESS TRAVELED

The Adirondack experience for walkers, hikers and climbers of all ages

New Enlarged Edition

Dennis Aprill

Illustrations by Sheri Amsel
Photographs by Dennis Aprill

Pinto Press
Mt. Kisco, NY

Portions of this book originally appeared in different form in the Plattsburgh *Press-Republican,* the Albany *Times-Union* and *Adirondack Life* magazine.

Book design by Dale Schroeder, Synergistic Data Systems
Cover design by Alison Muñoz
Photographs by Dennis Aprill

Publisher's Cataloging-in-Publication
(Provided by Quality Books, Inc.)

Aprill, Dennis.
    Paths less traveled : the Adirondack experience for walkers, hikers and climbers of all ages / Dennis Aprill ; illustrations by Sheri Amsel. — 2nd ed.
    p. cm.
    Includes bibliographical references.
    Preassigned LCCN: 00-131422
    ISBN: 0-9632476-9-7
        1. Hiking—New York (State)—Adirondack Mountains. 2. Mountaineer-ing—New York (State)—Adirondack Mountains. 3. Adirondack Mountains (N.Y.)—Guidebooks. I. Title.
GV199.42.N652A67 2000   796.51′1097475
                                    QBI00-434

10 9 8 7 6 5 4 3 2 1

Published by

Pinto 🐾 Press

Mt. Kisco, NY

Acknowledgments

The author would like to thank Joan and Roy Potter for their patience with me and enthusiasm for this book, and Bob Goetz, sports editor of the Plattsburgh *Press-Republican*, Mike Virtanen, features editor of the Albany *Times-Union*, and Betsy Folwell, *Adirondack Life* editor, for giving me initial support for writing about some of the climbs that were originally printed in their publications. To Sheri Amsel, Adirondack illustrator, my thanks for the use of her excellent drawings and her willingness to provide additional illustrations as needed.

To my children, Colin and Karalyn, thanks for being such great partners on the trails. And finally, thanks to my wife, Kathy, for her support, encouragement and fine proofreading, which kept my sentences from drifting off the trail.

Contents

Foreword

Welcome to the expanded edition of *Paths Less Traveled*. In it, I have added seven new mountains, including one that has been climbed by a person in a wheelchair. All are spread throughout the Adirondacks in keeping with the earlier edition, and all are relatively easy low-peak ascents. In fact, the average height of these new summits is 2,271 feet, the exact same average as the first 23 peaks.

After publication of the original *Paths Less Traveled*, I received letters and comments from readers who not only climbed the peaks described, but enjoyed keeping a log in the Diary Section. I've also gotten a lot of positive feedback from elderly climbers not up to the rigors of the High Peaks, and couples with young children who found these easier mountain climbs perfectly suited for their families. In all cases, the hikers I spoke with appreciated the uncrowded and unlittered trails. I hope, with this expanded edition, you will continue to enjoy the less-traveled paths. Maybe some day we will meet on the trail.

—Dennis Aprill
May, 2000

Kathy Aprill and friends hike on a path less traveled.

They are not cloud splitters, and you will not see them promoted in an "I Love New York" commercial. They are the mountains that peak baggers pass by on their way to becoming 46ers—people who have climbed the 46 highest peaks in the Adirondacks. You don't often look at breathtaking landscape photos of these hills, nor do you see crowds rushing to climb them, and that's their charm. These paths less traveled up the Adirondack low peaks are the focus of this book.

The 30 peaks described herein average 2,271 feet, less than half New York's highest mountain, Mount Marcy, at 5,280 feet. But elevation is relative to the surroundings, and these low mountains, though pint-sized, offer attractive views, often of the Adirondack or Catskill high peaks plus the myriad of ponds, lakes and forests that comprise the Adirondack Park.

Also, these mountains require much less effort to climb. Most of the trails to these summits are less than two miles long, and can be classed as moderate to moderately easy. The low peaks are perfect for families with children or for elderly mountaineers who can no longer muster the physical strength needed to climb the higher peaks.

Climbing the Adirondack low peaks has another advantage: because they are the paths less traveled, you don't have to put up with the crowds—some 200,000 climbers yearly in the High Peaks region alone! Most of these hikers enter through just a few trail heads, thus adding to the congestion.

The 30 mountains and hills described in my book were chosen because they offer good to great views from their summits, require

much less energy to climb than their higher cousins, give the hiker a degree of solitude, and are geographically spread throughout the Adirondack Park, with at least one peak in each of the ten Adirondack counties. To climb all 30 is to travel to the frontiers as well as the heartland of the Adirondacks.

The mountains described in this book are by no means the only low peaks in the Park that are worth climbing, and as time goes by, perhaps with reader feedback, more peaks will be added as new trails open up.

Paths Less Traveled is not meant to be a definitive work on climbing, nor a tenth-of-a-mile by tenth-of-a-mile description of trail conditions, but rather a guide to ex-

Even elderly hikers can enjoy climbing the Adirondack low peaks because, in general, the climbs are less challenging than those of their higher cousins. Here Dr. Adolph "Ditt" Dittmar, one of the original 46ers, hikes near Silver Lake Mountain.

periencing the natural wonders of the Adirondacks as you walk to the summits that I describe. Because these peaks can be climbed in an hour or two, there is no need to hurry to the top. I encourage you to enjoy the journey, bring along your field guides, and try to learn one new aspect of nature on each trip.

Much of the technical jargon found in more traditional trail guides is left out of *Paths Less Traveled.* It doesn't really matter if that lean-to is .25 miles from the sign-in register, only that you passed it and are on your way toward a climax hardwood forest, wet area, or clump of softwoods. Instead of third-person accounts like most trail guides, this book is written in the first person, so you are seeing the trail through my eyes. I have included a diary section of 46 pages, two for each climb, so you too can recount your experiences along the trails. These accounts can be reflected upon or shared in years to come.

To aid in your learning about these low peaks, I have added drawings by the Adirondack illustrator, Sheri Amsel, of relevant plants, animals, trees, birds, or important physical features you will see on your climb. I have also digressed from straight-line narrative at times to relate what I believe to be interesting historical and natural history anecdotes about the immediate area.

Aside from what is contained in the following chapters, I can offer a few additional tips: if you, like me, enjoy solitude, consider taking one of the climbs at midweek instead of on a weekend. If you make ascents during blackfly season, bring along a head net and lightweight gloves, and cover up with breathable clothing. (I have yet to find a repellent that works on blackflies.)

One of my favorite hiking seasons is in the fall from just after Labor Day to early October. The summer folks have departed; the leaf peepers have yet to arrive in hordes; the bugs are pretty much gone, and the days are still warm.

Whatever the season and whichever mountain you start with, I encourage you to make the most of the trip: stop, look around, listen to and smell the natural wonders surrounding you. Tread lightly on these paths less traveled and enjoy the journey.

Chapter 1

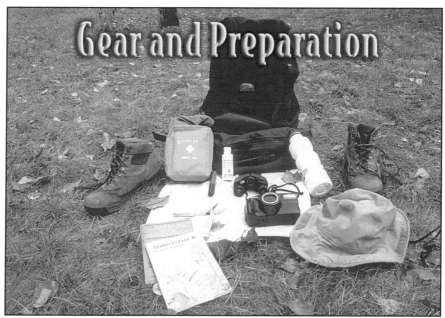

Some useful gear to carry along when climbing the low peaks.

Equipment needed to climb the low peaks can be as simple and unassuming as the mountains themselves. High-tech, state-of-the-art hiking boots, crampons or the latest breathable parkas are unnecessary; all that is required is some very practical gear that can be used on a variety of hikes.

Let's start with footwear. While many of these smaller mountains can, during the dry summer months, be climbed by someone wearing sneakers or running shoes, it is best to use some type of traditional hiking boot with Vibram soles for traction. I recommend Gore-Tex-lined hiking boots. They cost a little more, but will be greatly appreciated when you cross the muddy sections and small brooks on your climbs. Granted, when it comes to kids it's hard to reconcile spending a lot of money on a pair of boots they will surely outgrow in one season, and unless you have a younger child to wear them later on, the expense might not seem worth it. Even so, regular children's hiking boots, which are very lightweight, can be purchased for under $30, and they afford more support than sneakers.

Author with belt pack and two pouches attached to belt strap. One pouch carries a camera, the other miscellaneous items.

For winter travel, snowshoes are a must. The best ones come with metal frames, solid decking, and bindings with metal crampons, essential for climbing in deep or wet snow or slippery conditions. Some of the climbs described in this book, however, are not appropriate for winter ascents because of the short, steep rock climbing or close proximity to cliffs along the way. These should only be attempted by experienced winter climbers.

To carry my gear, I like a belt pack because its weight rests on the hips where it belongs, not on the shoulders like regular backpacks. In the belt pack goes juice or a canteen of water, lunch or a snack, a 35 mm camera and a couple of zoom lenses, and rain gear if wet weather is predicted. My best pack has straps attached to the top so an outer shirt can be tied on it after I shed it when I get too warm.

I have two pouches attached to the belt pack, similar to those used by hunters to carry bullets or muzzleloader gear. In one is my compact camera, a Nikon 800 autofocus. I keep it close at hand should I meet up with an interesting bird or animal. It has a lens that zooms from 37 to 105 mm. In the other pouch I carry a small first-aid kit, monocular, candy bar, compass and folded topo map.

Those who prefer day backpacks should get a small one with hip belt and sternum straps. Metal or plastic stays in the back help keep cargo such as cameras from hitting your back as you walk.

One other essential piece of outerwear is a hat, and I like a brimmed, Gore-Tex-lined one that breathes, sheds rain, and keeps off the horseflies. During blackfly season, I bring along a head net with black netting in the front for easier vision. Deciding between a head net or repellent is a personal choice, but I'd rather sweat a little than use a highly concentrated chemical.

As for conditioning, no special workout regimen is needed to get into shape to climb the low peaks. Of course, anyone with a heart problem or other potentially serious ailment should check with his or her doctor before starting to climb.

One good conditioner is a regular walking program that encompasses a variety of terrain. Speed is not the object here, just building a little endurance. Being in good condition makes these short climbs that much easier.

No matter how good shape you're in, don't overdo it. What's the hurry? You're not out there to "bag" peaks. You have all day, so slow down and enjoy the surroundings. On the steeper ascents, you may have to stop and catch your breath every 100 yards, or sometimes every 100 feet.

Finally, be careful on the descent. I believe more accidents occur on the way down the mountain than on the way up. It can be difficult putting on the brakes on a steep slope. Hold onto trees or rocks if necessary, and watch your step. As with the ascent, take your time going back downhill. If you do, it will make for a much more pleasant, memorable trip.

Chapter 2

Try to keep group size small when climbing paths less traveled. Group of six hikers shown rejoining after climbing Buck Mountain.

Etiquette, according to *Webster's Dictionary*, is "the forms, manners and ceremonies established by convention as acceptable." To take this definition a step further and apply it to hiking the low peaks, trail etiquette is behavior that doesn't despoil the landscape or ruin someone else's climb.

The first and most obvious thing hikers must do is carry out what they bring in and leave as little trace of their presence as possible. The novelty of the low peaks is their low usage; therefore, one individual dropping cigarette butts or food wrappers can ruin the experience for others. I will add here that just about all the 23 low-peak trails I traveled the past year were litter-free, a credit to the users.

Hikers should not leave calling cards—graffiti, initials on trees or stripped birch bark—along the way. One mountain that was not included in this book, though it met many of the criteria, is Rocky, near Inlet. The heavily used trail and summit have graffiti everywhere.

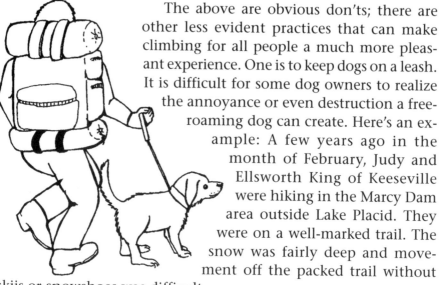

The above are obvious don'ts; there are other less evident practices that can make climbing for all people a much more pleasant experience. One is to keep dogs on a leash. It is difficult for some dog owners to realize the annoyance or even destruction a free-roaming dog can create. Here's an example: A few years ago in the month of February, Judy and Ellsworth King of Keeseville were hiking in the Marcy Dam area outside Lake Placid. They were on a well-marked trail. The snow was fairly deep and movement off the packed trail without skiis or snowshoes was difficult.

A small deer, after struggling through the powder, made it onto the trail in front of the Kings. As it did, it was attacked from the other direction by a dog wearing a collar. Before the Kings could reach the deer to help it, the dog had killed it and run off. The Kings, upset, continued on the trail. A quarter mile farther on they met up with a well-dressed, well-equipped, cross-country ski party. The same dog, its tail wagging, followed the group. The Kings tried to explain what had happened, but the group members refused to believe them. They couldn't fathom the fact that their lovable pet could do such a thing.

They are not alone. There is really no good reason to have a dog banging through the forest disrupting wildlife. Respect for other hikers, who may not be so enamored of dogs, should be enough incentive for hikers to leash their pets.

If possible, hike in small groups. The trails to these low peaks aren't hardened like some of the heavily used ones in the High Peaks region. Anyone who has been behind a small army heading up one of our popular mountains knows what it is like to encounter congestion in the back country.

Basically, trail etiquette, as described here, is a matter of common sense; respect the environment and fellow hikers so that everyone can enjoy the experience.

Chapter 3

Mother and daughter walking together, sharing experiences on the trail.

Having two children of my own hardly qualifies me as an expert on hiking with kids, so what follows is based on personal experience—trial and error—not on some advanced scientific research.

First, with kids under ten, keep expectations as low as the mountain you intend to climb, especially if you are with really young children who will be walking on their own the entire trip. The low peaks in this book are good starter mountains, particularly Sawyer, Coon and Severance Hill. Try not to set daunting goals for kids not used to serious mountain climbing. Take one mountain at a time and see how it goes.

Be sure to take it easy both climbing and descending the mountain. I have a tendency to walk fast. When I'm out with my kids, I try to cut my own pace in half, which isn't that difficult going uphill. Stay close to your son or daughter. There's nothing worse than having a discouraged child struggling a half mile behind, trying to keep up with you.

As I mentioned in a previous chapter, be careful on the descent, since I believe more accidents occur going downhill than up. Why?

Small group of children and adults hike together at start of trail up to Echo Cliffs near Piseco Lake.

Because everyone is tired at this point. We don't lift our feet as high and, therefore, are more likely to trip or slip. Running downhill, as kids like to do, increases the chance of injury.

Encourage your young companions. Stop frequently along the way, if necessary, for snacks or just to putter around. There are probably some interesting flowers, trees, rocks or animal tracks worth investigating along the way, so carry some field guides.

Bring along a small first-aid kit with plenty of Band-Aids. My son and daughter inevitably pick up some scrapes and cuts along the trail, and a quick Band-Aid application lifts spirits and morale.

Don't forget to carry some water, juice or your children's favorite drink in a canteen or plastic bottle. Climbing can create dry throats. Encourage them to wear hats; horseflies, in particular, can be tormenting during the summer months.

Be prepared for unexpected conditions. Bring along rain gear if there is a possibility of wet weather. Kids can get by with those cheap plastic ponchos that fold to the size of a calculator, but for more serious climbing, a two-piece nylon rainsuit is preferable.

Finally, put yourself in your kid's place. Realize that kids, with their shorter legs and smaller lungs, can't be expected to have the same stamina as adults. Ask yourself, if you were the child would you want to be out there with an adult who is impatient and in a hurry, or one who encourages and shares the experience with you? I believe most of us would choose the latter.

Almost there! Youngsters with parents near summit of Black Bear Mountain.

Thoughts About Climbing With Teens

Hiking with a teenager is quite different from hiking with a young child. For most young kids, the world of nature is a big amusement park full of new experiences. These positive experiences only need to be encouraged and nurtured.

Teens are a little more cynical. They are, in many cases, physically almost adult but very sensitive emotionally. Patience and understanding are the keys to a successful trip with a teen. For example, my 13-year-old son, Colin, went through a stage where he didn't want to walk with his parents at malls, so we expected the same on the trails. Surprisingly, away from the social element he did an about-face and kept up with us on all our climbs.

Teens have different needs and perspectives than younger children. Here, Colin Aprill, age 13, rests along Bear Mountain trail near Cranberry Lake.

Instead of some of the lighthearted things we discussed when he was six, we talked about the bigger picture on our climb of Bear Mountain. Near Cranberry Lake, for example, we discussed wolves, coyotes, deer and the role of hunting on the Adirondack deer herd. Colin has a great deal of interest in hunting, so we had a good conversation along the way.

With our teenager, my wife and I have tried to accentuate the positive and allow our son in on the decision making and trip planning. On our way home from a climb, we stop at a hamburger place or an eatery of his choice and relax for awhile. For many busy parents, going on climbs such as the low peaks may be some of the few times they get to spend an afternoon with their teenager.

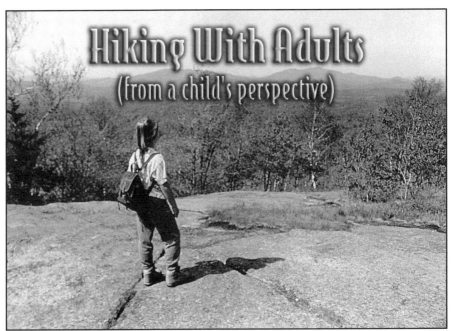

Chapter 4

Hiking With Adults
(from a child's perspective)

Karalyn Aprill, on Panther Mountain, equipped with small backpack filled with snacks and juice.

by Karalyn Aprill, age 10

I enjoy hiking with my dad. Over the years, we have climbed some very interesting mountains like Hadley, Cathead and Kane. They all have great views and fire towers that I wanted to climb up to the top.

My dad wouldn't let me go all the way up, though, because he's afraid of high places like tall fire towers, so he only let me climb part way up all of them except Kane. We both had to climb that one to see over the trees. When I do go up high in the tower, he yells, "Be careful!"

On the trail, my dad is good company, but sometimes he walks a little too fast. Now we have our own system when the climbing is steep: he walks, then rests while I catch up; then I get to rest.

I also like hiking with my entire family. My mother, father and brother Colin (age 13) and I hiked up Silver Lake Mountain last

Speed is not the goal in climbing the low peaks. Karalyn Aprill, shown here, tries to catch up with her father on the ascent of Cathead Mountain.

October. Even though it rained a little, the scenery was beautiful, but the trail was slippery and I had to hold on to trees on some steep sections.

Another bit of advice: it is best for parents not to push their kids too much. Some of us like to run ahead, then we tire out; others move slowly. We all like to run downhill, which can be dangerous. Talk to us and help us learn about new things.

We've seen a lot of neat things on our hikes. On Hadley, I caught an American toad and carried it all the way to the top. I then let it go. Dad won't let me keep

toads or newts that I find on the trail.

We always bring along lots of snacks that I like such as Airheads, fruit roll-ups, gum, peanut-butter sandwiches and, of course, juice.

The thing I like most about hiking with my dad is the attention I get. At home he has to spend time with Mom, my brother and me. On our trips, it's only me.

If I could give some advice to parents taking their kids hiking, I would say, "Slow down and bring them lots of snacks, and don't, like my dad does, put the oldies radio station on in the car on the trip to the mountain." That music drives me crazy! One other thing I would ask my dad: "Take me with you in the fall and spring so I can get out of school!!"

Chapter 5

During the summer, carpet moss blankets rocks.

Though the trails up the Adirondack low peaks remain pretty much the same over the years, the forests, plants and wildlife that live near them are ever-changing.

Spring is a relative term in northern New York, and its arrival time varies depending on where you live. In the Champlain Valley, for example, mountains like Coon and Cook could be snow-free by early April, while peaks to the west like Bald, Black Bear, Owls Head and Azure may still have some snow on their summits or along the paths to the summits into May.

I enjoy hiking in the early spring. Everything is fresh, new, growing—free from the bonds of winter's snow. Fiddlehead ferns are everywhere. Yellow trout lilies, violets and white hepatica extend their delicate flowers almost cautiously, as if hugging the brown forest floor. These early flowers add the first color of the season. Later, painted trilliums and the small white Canada mayflowers push up as spring progresses.

Climbing in spring is a wet affair. Waterproof, preferably Gore-Tex-lined, boots are a must. Trail sections are often slippery and

17

lady slipper

care should be taken when crossing bare ledges or leaf-covered rocks. Though it is tempting to make wide detours to avoid some of the puddles, fight the urge, since making paths off the trail causes erosion of delicate soil.

As May progresses and the poplars (popples) send out their baby green leaves, the blackflies arrive, first in small groups that don't bite; these are followed a week later by the hordes that are the scourge of outdoors folks. There is also beauty during fly season. Lady slippers, both pink and white, are in bloom as are bunchberries and wild cherries and apples.

Because the flies discourage hikers, this is a good time for those who seek solitude on the trail to get out and do a couple of climbs. Cover up, wear a head net and lightweight gloves. Blackflies must land on the skin and actually chew it in order to create irritation, unlike mosquitoes who can bore through clothing to draw blood from below the skin.

Also, the Neotropical birds, those that overwinter down south, are back, and the call of the robin in the meadows along with the flute-like song of the wood thrush in the forest are common sounds, for this is the height of the mating season for these birds.

By late June, the blackflies have pretty well died off and the warm days have begun. Along with summer come the crowds, who gravitate to popular hiking areas like the High Peaks. Hikes during July and August are often accompanied by sweating from heat and humidity. Heat waves can sometimes be seen dancing upon bare rock summits, and views may be clouded with mist. This is the season to wear hiking shorts, lightweight breathable tops, and broad-brimmed hats that protect you from the sun's rays. These hats also help shield you from the deerflies and horseflies that circle about like tiny alien spacecraft. The forests are a little quieter in summer, as the birds, exhausted by the mating season, are less talkative. Carpet moss covers rocks like a perfectly installed rug.

By Labor Day the summer season is winding down, and after this holiday right up until Columbus Day is my favorite time of year to climb. The days are still warm, the weather settled. The nights are cool with a touch of frost, and most of the bugs are gone. The leaf peepers have yet to arrive in large numbers, so there is ample opportunity for quiet, peaceful hikes. One's sense of smell is heightened during this season. Fallen leaves mix with rotting downed trees, soil, and the often numerous mushrooms to give off earthy scents. This is also the time when the first flocks of Canada geese fly overhead.

Fall offers its own intimacy, a time to reflect while on the trail.

There is a noticeable quiet in the late September woods. Maybe this is because many of the Neotropical birds have left. But there are subtle sounds, such as leaves filtering down through hardwoods. During this season if a blue jay squawks or a crow caws, you take notice as the cry breaks the silence.

At the trail heads and in open areas are purple asters and goldenrod. Monarch butterflies often pass through on their long journey to Mexico in late September. Their orange-and-black wings, so reflective of fall hues, add another splash of color to the already bright oranges, reds and yellows on the slopes.

November is another good month to climb the low peaks. The leaves are off the hardwoods, and this allows for better views. November weather often varies; snow, sleet and rain could all be falling in the same area, changing from one to the other with the altitude.

Winter climbs may be the most challenging, but offer an opportunity to observe the movements of wild animals through the tracks they leave in the snow.

In November the big game-hunting season is in full swing, but fear of being wounded by a stray bullet should not deter anyone from climbing mountains. Statistics show that non-hunters are rarely involved in hunting mishaps. Wear some bright orange clothing, stay on the trails and keep dogs leashed, which is a good practice year round.

When the snows arrive, usually in December, new opportunities open up for climbers. Animal tracks form mosaics on the white powder. After a big storm, snow builds up on small evergreens, forcing them to bend over. Stumps become giant white mushrooms. In the winter, there are even fewer sounds than in the fall, and very cold, clear days accentuate the stillness. The swishing sound that snowshoes make, or the explosion of a tree from frozen sap, are the few noises that break the winter silence.

Winter offers some of the more intimate yet demanding climbs, and beginners should try only the easiest mountains, like Sawyer and Severance Hill. Both can be either skied or snowshoed. Winter hikes require conditioning, the right clothing, worn in layers, and close attention to local weather conditions. There is no need to risk getting lost in a storm when the same mountain can be climbed another day. After all, these mountains will be around for a long, long time.

Adirondack Park Map

The circled numbers indicate the chapters for each mountain.

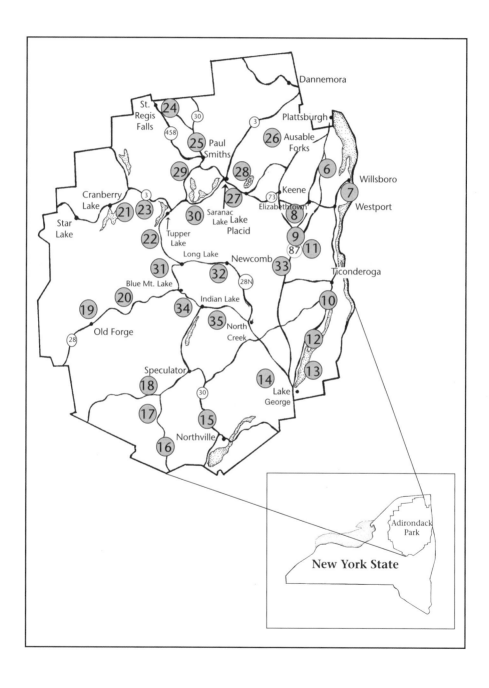

Chapter 6

View from summit looking west with Whiteface Mountain in center.

The massive cliffs of Poke-O-Moonshine Mountain, standing as a rugged gateway to the Adirondacks for those heading south on the Northway, dominate the surrounding area. These cliffs are like a fortress at the mountain range's northern frontier, so distinctive that they can be seen for miles from both the north and south.

For decades I have admired the magnificent cliffs that front this 2,180-foot mountain. I had been tempted to climb the mountain many times, but those intimidating vertical sheets of rock put me off. Last fall all that changed when I pulled in at the state campsite off Route 9, three miles south of the Northway's Exit 33.

I found no designated parking area, so I just pulled over to one side of Route 9 and walked through the campsite to where a DEC yellow-on-brown sign pointed to the 1.2-mile-trail up the mountain.

The morning was cool and crisp, a perfect day to climb a mountain. Added to the ideal weather was the fact that, after checking the sign-in register, I discovered that I would be the first one up there that day.

The dominant cliffs that front Poke-O-Moonshine.

The trail rises immediately and is well worn, cutting through a hardwood forest of beech, red maple, and some yellow birch. Violets and trout lilies that poked their tiny flowers out in the spring now made lovely green borders with their leaves. After about a half mile of steady uphill work, I came to an opening on the right side of the trail. A short spur trail led to cliffs and views to the north and east. Below, Route 9 and Northway traffic moved along, creating a muffled rumbling sound. To the left, the cliff above was a mix of smooth and broken rock. I figured this was the part of the cliffs visible from the highways below.

The cliffs of Poke-O-Moonshine are about 1,000 feet high and are favorites of rock climbers. They are made of granite gneiss, a course-grained rock that is composed of alternating layers of different minerals. It is very resistant to weathering. Some geologists believe there is a fault line near the base of the cliffs.

The cliffs are home to one of the few nesting pairs of peregrine falcons in New York. To protect the falcons's nest, the Department of Environ-

violet

Steep, rocky section on Poke-O-Moonshine climb.

mental Conservation has closed parts of the cliffs to rock climbers. If hikers see a crow-sized bird, slate blue-black above and white on the underside, soaring in front of the cliffs, they are asked to report their sightings to the nearest DEC wildlife office.

After a few minutes on the spur trail, I returned to the main trail and continued up over sheer rock that was slippery in sections. A good pair of hiking boots is an asset here. In places the ascent can only be described as steep, and I took frequent rest stops. Finally, I reached the site of the fire-tower keeper's cabin, or rather its remains: foundation pilings and stone chimney.

peregrine falcon

From here it was a short climb to the top, then more walking to where the trees cleared and the old fire tower appeared. And what a view! In the foreground looking east were the highways, but farther to the northeast two bodies of water—Augur Lake and Butternut Pond—stood out clearly. Off in the distance I saw what at first looked like the horizon; then it began to take shape. I realized it was Lake Champlain shrouded in mist as the cold night air had mixed with the warmer water. As I walked toward the cliff and glanced to the right, I saw Whiteface Mountain on the horizon to west.

Behind me the old fire tower stood, the first flight of steps removed. Today there are no state fire wardens, and some towers are scheduled for removal because they do not conform to the state master plan for wilderness-designated areas. Those towers, like Poke-O-Moonshine's, that are on "wild forest" designated land can remain, but need volunteers to refurbish and care for them. Towers on Hadley Mountain, in the southern Adirondacks, and Blue Mountain have sponsors. The tower on Owls Head near Long Lake does not.

After an hour of puttering around and picture taking, I headed down the mountain, a trip that was as difficult as the climb. Often on the way down, hikers are tired and more apt to stumble over rocks or roots. Every hiker has his or her own way of working through steep sections; mine is to place my feet sideways against the ground and lean toward the slope, inching through really rough sections. Handy branches, saplings and trees can help keep one afoot.

When I got back to the campsite, no other cars were parked there. I was still the only climber that day. In fact, judging from the sign-in book, there had been only a couple of climbers all week.

On my way home, I first drove south to get a glimpse of the tower on Poke-O-Moonshine. It looked even more impressive atop that mass of stone when viewed from below, now that I had just experienced the scenes from the top.

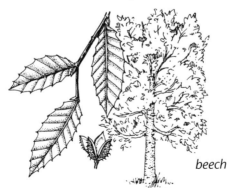

beech

To Get There

Take Northway (I-87) exit to Route 9 and its intersection with Route 22. Drive south three miles to a state campsite on right. Park safely off main highway. Trail is at the end of the campsite. A yellow-on-brown DEC sign points the way.

Technical Information
Height: 2,180'
Trail length: 1.2 miles
Difficulty: Fairly difficult

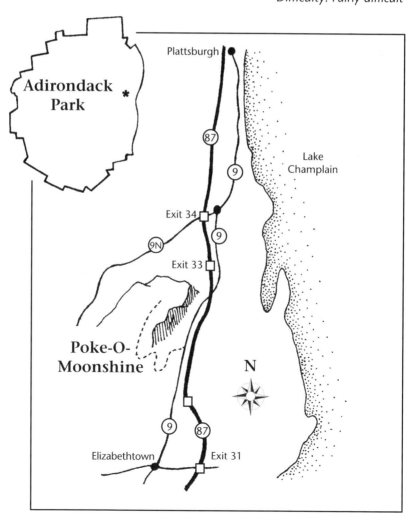

Chapter 7

Northwest Bay of Lake Champlain seen from Coon Mountain.

For me and my daughter, Karalyn, climbing Coon Mountain in central Essex County in the month of April can best be summed up this way: rarely have we exerted so little effort for such a great return—the peak's magnificent views.

Coon Mountain sits just west of Split Rock and Lake Champlain. It is owned by the Adirondack Land Trust. The Nature Conservancy maintains a trail to the summit of this modest 1,000-foot peak.

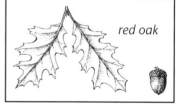

red oak

From the parking area, just off Halds Road near Wadhams, we climbed through a young forest of hardwoods that included red oak, yellow birch, and sugar maple. Apparently the area had been logged at one time, since the trail started at an old skid road.

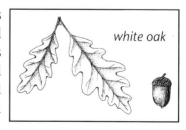

white oak

29

Karalyn hiking by the anorthosite cliffs.

Trail markers were scarce along the entire one-mile climb, with only two signs pointing direction. It was a matter of locating and staying on the beaten path. Early on, don't follow the red markers on trees; they are not trail markers, but property line demarcations.

The climb was easy until we came to a ravine two-thirds of the way up. Here, a rock slide, brook, or some other natural phenomenon had created a valley of boulders. The trail hugged the left side, but Karalyn, a typical 10 year old, preferred using the rocks as steps. This is a section where you should take your time to avoid nasty falls.

After the ravine, the trail skirts some quite impressive cliffs of anorthosite, an ancient rock that underlies much of the Adirondacks. Near the top, small white flowers—hepaticas, one of the first of the early spring blooms—poked their fragile heads above the mulch. Finally, after less than 30 minutes, we reached the summit, and what a view!

To the west were the High Peaks—Dix, Giant, and Hurricane—still covered with snow. To the south was Northwest Bay of Lake Champlain, mist rising from the surface of the big lake and evaporating as it lifted upward. Because the foliage wasn't out yet, we could see to the northwest

toward Whiteface and northeast up Lake Champlain into Vermont. In all, our view was about 300 degrees of open vistas.

The top of Coon Mountain is open rock with some juniper and softwoods. While we rested and snacked, I read the Nature Conservancy brochure that tells of two legends associated with the mountain.

The first involves William Gilliland, an original settler in the area for whom Willsboro is named. He was a wealthy man until the Revolutionary War, after which he lost almost every-

On the trail to the summit

thing. In 1796, broke and alone, Gilliland got lost and died on the mountain.

Another legend revolves around the Coon Mountain panther. It was said that this big cat cried like a damsel in distress, luring people into the woods for its next meal. The panther was finally shot as it leaped off one of the many cliffs, its body falling into a tarn, a hole with water at the bottom. The panther was never found; some believe its spirit still haunts Coon Mountain.

On our descent, Karalyn and I didn't see any ghosts or panthers, just a couple of chipmunks and two deer at the trail head. But we did come away with memories of a very enjoyable, easy climb. Although we made the ascent of Coon Mountain in less than half an hour, more time should be allowed for a leisurely hike.

To Get There

To get to the Coon Mountain trail head, take the Northway (I-87) to Exit 31, and turn onto Route 9N east. Drive a very short distance to Youngs Road on the left. Take this road to Wadhams.

From Wadhams, drive north on Route 22 to the well-marked Merriam Forge Road turnoff on the right. Follow this road that crosses, then parallels the Boquet River for 1.5 miles until the Halds Road cutoff on the left. The trail head is one mile down Halds Road; the parking area is on the left.

Technical Information
Height: 1,000'
Trail Length: One mile
Difficulty: Moderately easy

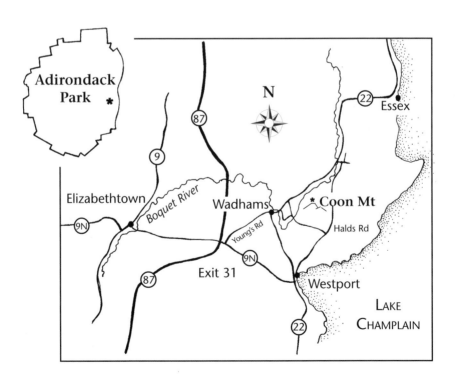

Chapter 8

From atop Baxter Mountain looking east toward Elizabethtown.

Baxter Mountain is an unassuming nub dwarfed by the Adirondack High Peaks to its west and Giant Mountain to its southeast. Yet this 2,440–foot summit provides excellent views of some of these well-known mountains and a lot more. One Monday in late November I pulled over to the side of Route 9N, two miles from its intersection with Route 73, and began the 1.1–mile hike to the top of Baxter.

The trail, which is marked by ADK signs, at first weaves through small softwoods like white pine and balsam, then crosses a power line cut. The ascent was gradual, the trail relatively dry considering the very wet fall weather that year. Unlike many well-used Adirondack trails, there were no massive roots protruding out of the dirt like groping tendrils, indicating its hard-packed surface.

The morning was overcast, with rain threatening, but the forecasts

Juniper

Trail up Baxter is hard-packed dirt with occasional boulders.

were for clearing skies. I hoped those predictions would come true, as I wanted to get some good photo shots of the High Peaks and Keene Valley below.

About a third of the way up the mountain, the softwoods gave way to a more mature white birch and beech forest, and the ascent became steeper. In one place, I saw fresh fox tracks. I assumed them to be made by the red version because gray fox prefer lower terrain hardwood forests. These two types of foxes differ in that the gray is the only North American canine that can climb trees. While the gray's distribution in the North Country is limited, the red fox can be found in a variety of habitats.

After stepping over a blown-down poplar that crossed the trail, which at this stage was more like a narrow path, the steep climb continued on smooth rock shelves. I grabbed nearby roots and saplings as I worked upward, finally coming out above a bare rock cliff near the summit.

Red
Fox

Below, I saw where a house was being constructed near Beede Ledge, but that was

Trailhead off Route 9N east of Keene.

the only sign of civilization to the south. I climbed farther and was rewarded with my first glimpse of the Keene Valley to the west and the Great Range of the High Peaks beyond that. Clouds hovered above the highest peaks, looking very much like a major high country snowstorm was brewing, yet the temperature at the trail head was in the 50s. To the east, a valley curved toward Elizabethtown.

Growing all about the summit of Baxter are blueberry plants and juniper bushes; the latter were still covered with berries though the bushes themselves were a deep yellow. Scattered red pines and saplings broke up the otherwise moss-and-lichen-covered rock.

After a half-hour of taking in the scenery and waiting for the clouds to break, I finally decided to head down, figuring any weather changes that day were going to occur slowly. On my return, I took it easy over the steep sections. I'm convinced they are more dangerous on the descent when you're tired and expecting an easier stretch.

But in 30 minutes I was back at my truck, and while driving home on Route 9N in Keene, the sun finally broke through the clouds. This bad timing, however, didn't dampen what was a very relaxed and solitary climb up a little mountain that offers some great views of Keene Valley and the higher mountains beyond it.

To Get There

From the intersection of Routes 73 and 9N about two miles south of Keene, take Route 9N uphill for two miles. The Baxter trail head is on the right just past the Hurricane Mountain Road (on left). There is no formal parking area, just pull off the road and begin the climb.

Technical Information
Height: 2,440
Trail Length: 1.1 mile
Difficulty: Moderate

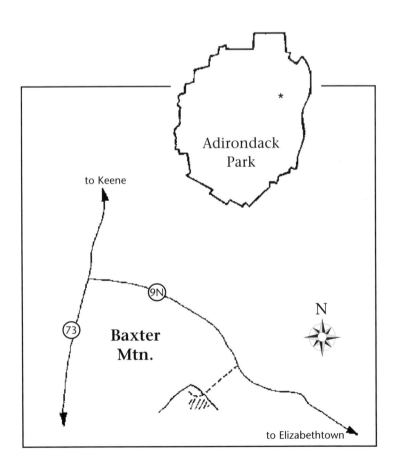

Chapter 9

Scene from atop Belfry, looking west toward the High Peaks.

On an early October Saturday morning, 10-year-old Brennan Hathaway performed a remarkable feat. With the help of his grandparents, Leanna and Dick DeNeale from Willsboro, Brennan climbed Belfry Mountain in his wheelchair.

Almost there, Dick DeNeale pushes grandson Brennan up Belfry Mountain.

Belfry itself is also remarkable in that this small mountain, arguably the easiest climb in the Adirondacks, provides excellent views of Lake Champlain to the east, the High Peaks to the west, the Pharoah Lake Wilderness to the south, and even Whiteface to the

37

north. There is a fire tower atop Belfry that adds even more scenic possibilities, but that additional effort isn't necessary to get enjoyment from this mountain.

The story behind Brennan's climb and my role in all this is an interesting one. A month earlier I had climbed Belfry and had written about my experiences in a newspaper article. I told of how, from the trail head, a mere roadside pullover near Mineville

PhotoCourtesy Leanna DeNeale

Grandfather and grandson take in scenery atop Belfry.

marked by a yellow gate, I made the leisurely .4 mile walk through a mixed hardwood forest. The dirt road was hard-packed and without major obstacles.

After passing a large antenna receiver on the right, I came out on the bare rock 1,820-foot summit where I alone surveyed the sights. Besides the panorama of lake and mountains in the distance, I saw Mineville, Moriah and in the foreground the remains of iron mines closed for decades.

Snow Goose

After taking in all these sights, I returned to my car and later wrote the article that was published the next week. A couple of days after that, Leanna called and asked if I thought their grandson Brennan would be able to make this climb. She told me, "Early on we used to take him up Baxter and Noonmark Mountains. He enjoyed coming with us even when we carried him as a baby." She added that Brennan had been diagnosed with muscular dystrophy a couple of years ago and eventually, after losing muscle control, had no choice but to use a wheelchair.

I informed her about the trail conditions, but admitted that I had no experience with handicapped hikers. But, I told her, "Why not give it a try?"

Lincoln Pond, with state-run campsites and boating.

Two weeks later Brennan and the DeNeales made their re-markable climb up Belfry Mountain. Leanna and Dick pulled their van over near the beginning of the trail and lifted the boy down. As his grandfather pushed the chair, Brennan helped out by turning the wheels with his hands—they did not use an electric wheel-chair. When they reached the summit, Brennan's reaction was like that of any young climber: "The views were great! I'm glad we tried it."

In this era of concern for those who are physically challenged having the op-portunity to enjoy outdoor experiences within their capabilities, Brennan's trek up Belfry Mountain shows that such ex-periences can be had if you know where to look. As Leanna said, "It is nice to have a mountain everyone, regardless of physi-cal ability, can enjoy." Certainly Belfry comes the closest to this ideal than any other Adirondack Mountain I've seen.

Service Berry

To Get There

Take Northway Exit 30 a short way to Route 9 and make an almost immediate left onto County Route 6. Go down this road 8 miles to a four-way intersection. Turn left onto County Route 70 and drive up a grade .6 mile, the yellow gate marking the trail head is on the left.

From Elizabethtown, take Route 9 to where County Route 7 forks to the right just outside town. This road skirts Lincoln Pond (campsite, fishing and boating available), then rises to a "Y." Take the right (sign pointing to Witherbee) which is County Route 70. The trail head is .5 mile beyond.

Technical Information
Height: 1,820 feet
Trail Length: .4 mile
Difficulty: Easy

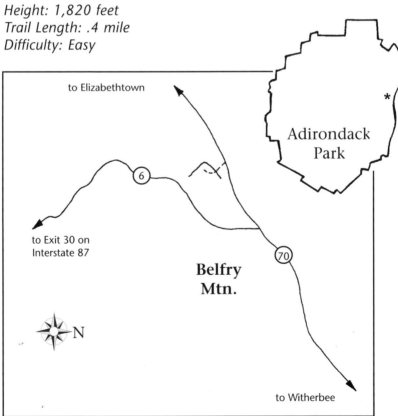

The northern end of Lake George from atop Cook Mountain; unlike the southern section, this end shows little or no development.

Cook Mountain sits just south of Ticonderoga and a little west of Lake George. It has watched over many historic struggles between the British, French, and Americans for control of upstate New York.

Lake George, the largest lake in the Adirondack Park, was named Lac du Saint Sacrement by a Jesuit missionary named Father Isaac Jogues when he saw it for the first time in 1642. It was renamed Lake George in 1755 by British General William Johnson in honor of King George II. Major battles of the French and Indian War and the American Revolution were fought here. Today, a relatively new trail goes to the top of this low peak, making it and the views it offers accessible to the public.

The mountain and adjoining lowlands are part of a large estate that once belonged to a family named Cook. George Delano, a Civil War veteran injured in the Battle of Harpers Ferry, bought the 176-acre parcel on and around the mountain in 1876. His descendants, Donald and Marjorie Delano, gave the land to the Lake George

Trail up Cook starts in meadow off Baldwin Road south of Ticonderoga.

Basin Land Conservancy in 1990. Since then, an additional 18 acres have been added to the preserve.

In mid-June, with my regular hiking companion—my daughter, Karalyn—I climbed this 1,200-foot peak. The trail head lies just off Baldwin Road. There is no parking area; we just pulled off the side of the road where there is a locked gate and a sign-in box.

At first we walked near a wetland created by extensive beaver works. Then the trail rises gradually through a forest of tall hardwoods. Here, horsetails—primitive ferns that appear light and airy— grow on both sides of the old jeep trail.

After one-half mile, the trail comes to a junction; the path to the right (yellow markers) goes to the beaver ponds, while the other makes a sharp left and climbs steadily. At this point, we began our ascent.

Stunted red oaks dominate Cook Mountain summit.

We worked our way up small ridges, in some places fairly steep, through a forest of maple, beech and oak, until the trail leveled off at about a mile. Besides red oak, common in the Adirondack foothills, white oak and chestnut oak grow on the slopes of Cook. The latter two are uncommon in the mountains. Our respite was short-lived; soon we began climbing again, finally reaching a small plot of white pines mixed in with oak and bare rock. This was our first chance to take a glance at the valley below.

Interestingly, the oak, as we approached the summit, were all stunted and looked very much like the pruned, evenly spaced trees seen at an apple orchard. According to the Conservancy brochure: "This south-facing slope composes a rocky-summit grassland community that experiences climatic extremes that hinder the growth of shrubs and trees."

chestnut oak

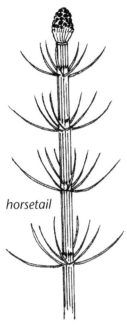

horsetail

The day we were there, strong southern winds blew up the Lake George Valley, cooling us and keeping the flies and mosquitoes at bay. At the summit, 1.7 miles from our start and 865 feet higher up, we were rewarded with a great view of the northern end of Lake George with Rogers Rock in the foreground, the Tongue, a massive rock mountain, behind it, and the Green Mountains of Vermont for a backdrop.

We could only imagine that in the spring, before the oaks leaf out and block some of the vistas, Mount Defiance and Mount Independence, which surround Fort Ticonderoga, and the southern sections of Lake Champlain, 200 feet lower than Lake George, would also be visible.

On our descent, we took it easy through the steep sections. As we hiked down Cook Mountain, I reflected on the fact that this northern half of Lake George, from our vantage point, had no development to be seen, and probably looked very much like it did in colonial times.

To Get There

From the south, take Northway Exit 25 and travel east on Route 8 to Route 9N at Hague. Drive north on Route 9N into Ticonderoga to a four-way intersection with an historic monument in the center. Drive south down Lord Howe Street .75 mile to a stop sign. Turn left on Alexandria Street, then take an immediate right on Baldwin. The trail to Cook Mountain is 1.5 miles on the right.

From the north, take Northway Exit 31 to Route 9N east to Westport, then 9N/22 south to Ticonderoga. Continue on as described above.

Technical Information
Height: 1,200'
Trail length: 1.7 miles
Difficulty: Moderate

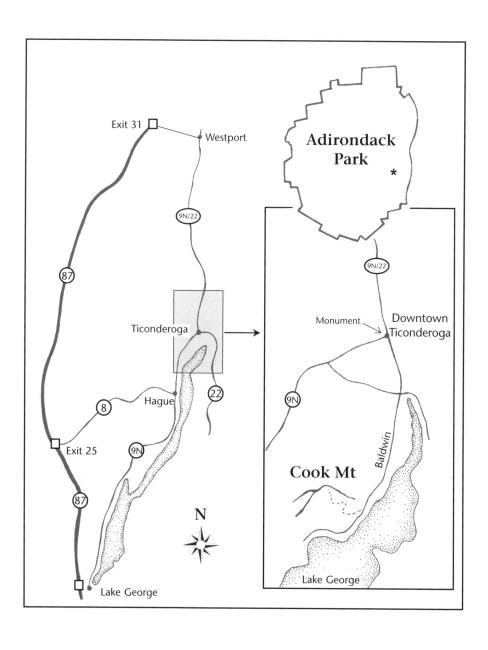

Chapter 11

15-year-old Colin Aprill rests near summit of Treadway Mountain.

About 15 minutes from the top of Treadway Mountain, my 15-year-old son, Colin, and I sat down, or rather collapsed, on a bare rock slab for a breather. Though only 2,248 feet high, Treadway, on that hot, steamy mid-July day, had extracted what felt like a gallon of sweat from us. But we soon found out that it was a worthwhile sacrifice for the views we would be treated to on the summit.

After drinking some water, we picked ourselves up for the final ascent, following rock cairn markers set on bare rock. Even on that hazy day, the views that unfolded were impressive, revealing at first the vague outline of the Tongue Mountain range to the southeast and an endless forest dotted with lakes of the Pharaoh Lake Wilderness Area below us. Treadway sits in the middle of this wild tract of land. Geographically speaking, we were roughly midway between Schroon Lake and Lake George, a perfect vantage for viewing the southeastern Adirondacks. Even our trip to the trail head was an adventure— we canoed there.

One way to get to Treadway Mountain is to canoe across Putnam Pond as author and his son did.

Actually, there are a number of ways to get to Treadway Mountain; the easiest starts at Putnam Pond State Campground in the Town of Ticonderoga. Here, we parked and unloaded our canoe for a short .6 mile paddle across the lake, almost due west, past two small peninsulas and down a bay to where the red-marked trail begins. Those not wanting to boat or canoe over can take the marked Grizzle Ocean Trail (yes, that's its name, though the small pond it leads to is anything but an ocean) that goes around Putnam from the parking area, adding 1.5 miles to the hike.

From where we beached our canoe, it's a 2.5 mile climb to the highest point on the main Treadway summit. We started on a well-worn, clearly marked trail that, after a short distance, circles Mud Pond, which empties into Putnam. In sections, roots and rocks seemed to reach out to trip us, but, due to the drought-like conditions that early July, most wet spots were dried mud. The forest we hiked through is a mix of hardwoods and balsam and hemlocks.

From here, we went uphill very gradually until our path joined with a yellow-and-blue trail. Then the red trail cut to the left, circling a small bog. We then made a couple of stream crossings on log bridges as we walked toward a small draw that drains into a

On approaching the summit of Treadway, the trail becomes bare rock marked by rock cairns.

pond called Devil's Washbasin. At this point, the trail became steeper, going from thick forest to open rock. I later learned the top of Treadway had burned in 1910. That explained why there were only scattered trees still trying to reclaim the once-scorched rock; however, there were blueberries everywhere.

Because of the heat and humidity, we rested often. The constant buzzing of horseflies and deerflies swooping down at us made these rest stops a little shorter than we had hoped. A hat was a necessity on a day like this. I wore my usual wide-brimmed hiking hat; Colin relied on his baseball cap. Back up and on the trail again, we were beginning to get our first glimpse, albeit a limited one, of the Champlain Valley off to the east.

There are actually three little knobs on the top of Treadway, with the third one, the last on the trail, providing the best views. We moved in that direction, the surrealistic mingling of mountains and forest unfolding through the haze: Blue and Snowy Mountains off to the far west, the Green Mountains of Vermont to the east, Moose and Crane Mountains to the south, and the Adirondack High Peaks to the northwest.

The day we climbed Treadway, July 1, Colin and I were the only hikers on the mountain, even though it was the day before a big July 4 weekend. It was like having our own private mountain to explore.

On our return, we relished the paddle back to the boat launch, the breeze keeping the flies at bay and providing a cool respite to what had been a demanding, though rewarding, climb up Treadway Mountain.

To Get There

Take Northway Exit 28 which leads to Route 74. Go east 12.5 miles to the yellow-on-brown DEC sign for the Putnam Pond State Campground turnoff on the right. The parking area is 3.5 miles down this road.

For Further Exploration: Putnam Pond

Putnam Pond, which we paddled, has designated campsites ($9.00 per night) on its shore and a beach for swimming. Day use fee is $5. Boats are available at the launch and can be rented for $10 half-day and $12 full-day. Putnam is stocked with tiger muskellunge and also has northern pike, yellow perch and smallmouth bass.

For reservations, call 1-800-456-2267; the caretaker's number is 518-585-7280.

Technical Information
Height: 2,248
Trail Length: 2.5 miles
Difficulty: Moderately Difficult

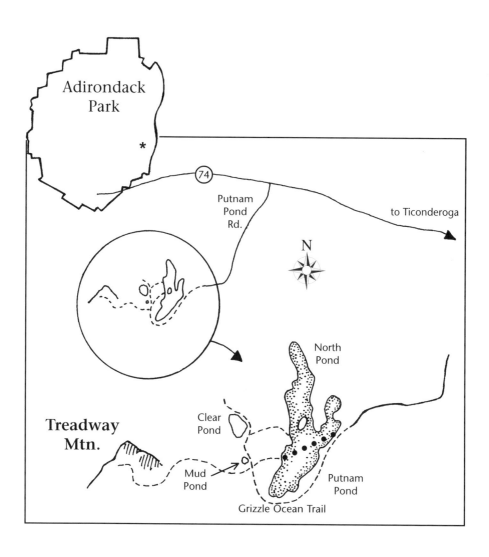

Chapter 12

View from Five Mile Mountain.

Five Mile Mountain lies deep in the heart of the Tongue Range, mountains aptly named because they jut into the center of Lake George like a lengthy tongue, separating Northwest Bay from the Lake George Narrows.

I climbed Five Mile in late October, following a 3.6-mile trail that actually crosses two different mountains—Brown and Five Mile—on its way south to the end of the Tongue Range at the peninsula's lower point. With snow in the air and more cold, damp weather predicted, I set limited goals: climb Brown and Five Mile, then return to the parking area off Route 9N, 9.5 miles north of Bolton Landing.

I had chosen that late date for a couple of reasons: most of the leaves would be off the hardwoods, affording more extensive views, and the timber rattlesnakes that make their home in the Tongue Range would be in their dens. Timber rattlers are a threatened species in New York and are not plentiful anywhere in the northern part of the state. One of their last strongholds is the Tongue.

The trail begins across Route 9N from the parking area. Early on, I saw signs that a large animal had been dragged along the trail.

A bare hardwood forest.

Bare dirt, then clumps of pine needles plus occasional deer hairs on rocks indicated that a successful hunter had been up in these mountains recently.

At .6 mile, the trail branches, the left fork heading to Deer Leap, a mile away and a perfect side trip. The lookout offers great views of Lake George to the southwest, including islands and mountains in the distance. The walk to Deer Leap is an easy one with little climbing.

About one mile beyond the fork, I saw something bright up ahead in a stand of hardwoods. It was a hunter dressed almost completely in colorful orange garb. We talked briefly, then I went on my way. Since non-hunters are rarely wounded in a hunting accident, don't be apprehensive about hiking during the big game season. To assure your safety, wear some bright orange clothing, even just a cap or vest; stay on the trail, and don't let pet dogs run free. Roaming dogs, mistaken for coyotes, have sometimes been shot.

On short climb from where the hunter stood, I passed through large stands of hemlocks, their spills making a soft, carpet-like surface. Then the trail rose again to the summit of Brown Mountain, about a mile and a half from the trail head. Brown's summit is tree-covered and offers no real views, just a few glimpses of Lake George through the hardwoods.

Lean-to with cairn in front.

After descending Brown, I hiked along a relatively level ridge for about a half mile. The forests alternated between hemlocks, white pines and birches, poplars and other hardwoods. A mile from Brown, the trail climbs steeply, reaching bare rock where only reindeer lichens and blueberries survive. Here, cairns—heaps of stones—spring up like permanent sculptures, not only for trail markers, it seems, but for would-be Rodins to display their creations. In one spot I counted 12 of these backwoods works of art. In the midst of the cairns is a lean-to. I had reached the 2.7-mile mark.

From the lean-to, which looked as if it hadn't been used for years, the trail alternated between downhill and uphill stretches with a few sharp turns thrown in until, in under a half mile, I reached another sign. It indicated the direction and distance—.45 mile—to Five Mile's summit. On the final climb, I passed cliffs, small pools of water hugging the side of the path, and more reindeer lichen and blueberries.

When I reached the first of the three lookout points, I saw a limited view to the north, with Lake George in the foreground. From the second lookout, a short walk farther, Black Mountain dominated the landscape with a small sliver of water below revealing the Lake George Narrows. The best views were at the third lookout. I

Rock cairns on lichen-covered rock near Five Mile summit.

saw Lake George to the south, and the outlines of mountains broke through the snowy air. In fact, there was snow cover on both Brown and Five Mile mountains.

As I photographed the scenery, things began to come unraveled. As anyone who travels the backwoods knows, mechanical equipment often quits at the wrong time and place. First, my Canon AE1 camera battery died and, of course, I had no spare. Then, my pocket Nikon 800 would not load film. Out came the Leatherman, a folding, multi-tool gadget, to crop the film. Finally, the camera took the roll and I continued to shoot pictures.

After about 20 minutes, I took stock and headed back to the trail head. But roughly three-quarters of a mile down, I felt for my Leatherman; it wasn't in its sheath. I had left it on the mountaintop. So, back up I went and found it lying where I had cropped the film.

On my final descent, I was alone; the hunter was gone. I had been the only person that day to climb the 2,256-foot Five Mile Mountain, a relatively low peak. It is an unusual mountain, since parts of it look like northern Canada, with lichens, pines and bare rock, and yet there are timber rattlesnakes, a more southern species, slithering about.

Timber Rattlesnakes of the Tongue

These large, poisonous snakes, some reaching six feet long, are listed by the Department of Environmental Conservation as "threatened" in New York State. The remote stretches of the Tongue Range make perfect homes for these reclusive reptiles.

Timber rattlers are long-lived, reaching maturity at eight to ten years of age. Some live up to 20 or 30 years. Females, however, breed only once every three years after they reach maturity.

According to DEC Reptile and Amphibian Specialist Al Breisch, the main food for timber rattlers on the Tongue is chipmunks, but they also eat squirrels, mice and other small mammals. Timber rattlesnakes mate in late summer, and winter in communal dens. Breisch thinks there are ten dens in the Tongue, with one housing as many as 100 snakes. Most of the dens, usually in rock crevices, are smaller.

In May, timber rattlers awaken from hibernation, bask in the spring sunshine, and, as the weather warms up, start moving about. Some males may travel two to three miles from their den. Breisch says there have been reports of rattlers swimming in Lake George. Campers have also sighted timber rattlesnakes on some of the Lake George Narrows islands.

Breisch says the snakes are not dangerous, with no reports of a hiker being bitten by one since the 1970s. If confronted, a timber rattler will curl up. When this happens, says Breisch, it is best to walk around it, giving it a lot of space. The snake is more afraid of you than you are of it.

To Get There

Take the Northway to Exit 24. Drive east 5.4 miles to Bolton Landing. Take Route 9N north 9.5 miles to the well-marked yellow-on-brown DEC sign indicating the trail and parking area.

Technical Information
Height: 2,256'
Trail Length: 3.6 miles
Difficulty: Moderate

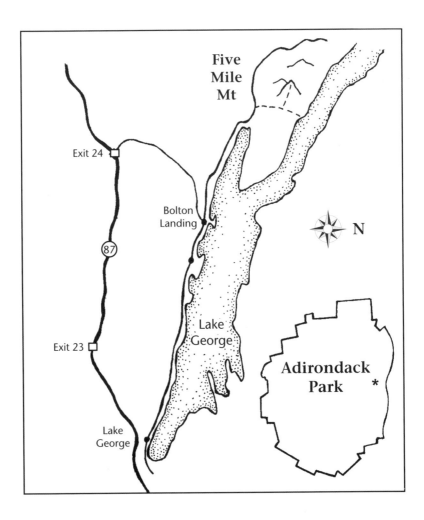

Chapter 13

The Tongue Range and Northwest Bay from Buck.

Lake George has often been described by writers, poets and painters as America's most beautiful lake. When he viewed it in 1791, Thomas Jefferson described it this way: "Lake George is, without comparison, the most beautiful water I ever saw; formed by a contour of mountains into a basin thirty-five miles long, and from two to four miles broad, finely interspersed with islands, its water limpid as crystal..."

Who could argue with Jefferson? With mountains rising from clear water that stretches to the horizon, the big lake is an impressive sight. And what could be a better way to observe this expansive body of water than from atop a mountain looking down, as I did at the height of the fall foliage season. From the summit of Buck Mountain, on the east side of Lake George, I was rewarded with truly great views of this magnificent lake and the multicolored mountains beyond it.

There are two trails up Buck Mountain. The more popular one starts at Highway 9L and is 3.3 miles long; the shorter, less-traveled

Tour boat on Lake George cruises north toward Bolton Landing.

One of many small brooks that must be crossed during the eastern ascent of Buck Mountain.

trail that I chose begins at a parking area off Butternut Falls Road. The state sign lists the distance as 2.5 miles; guidebooks calculate it as 2.3 miles.

From the parking area, where New England asters were the last of the flowers in bloom, I crossed a small brook, the first of seven streams I had to ford along the way. The trail then rises into a glen of tall hemlocks, their spills padding the pathway. That day also marked the first real cold spell of the season, and rolling gray clouds accompanied by a stiff breeze suddenly sent down a volley of hail. Then the sky cleared as I continued to climb through forests that alternated between hardwoods and hemlocks.

From bare rock summit of Buck looking southwest.

This trail up Buck is a wet one, which makes wearing a good pair of waterproof or Gore-Tex-lined boots a must. After crossing the last of the brooks, the trail turns steeply to the summit, following a tumbling stream uphill.

Just shy of the peak, I walked through a corridor of boulders before coming upon two signs. One pointed to Pilot Knob, a climb on the eastern shore, and the other indicated the summit of Buck, a short distance to the right.

As I reached the top, I was bowled over, literally, by the heavy winds sweeping up the valley. On that exposed summit of sheer rock, almost any piece of lightweight gear would have been blown away if not battened down. But the views were spectacular.

Looking to my right, I could clearly see Northwest Bay, the Tongue Range, and the Narrows. Beyond the Narrows, a portion of the wider part of the big lake near Hague glistened in the noonday sun. To the west was Bolton Landing and the Adirondacks beyond. Through the stiff wind I heard honking from above as a flock of Canada geese, the first I had seen that fall, flew overhead.

To the southwest, off in the distance, I thought I could recognize the outline of Hadley Mountain. Up the lake below chugged a tour boat, continuing a tradition of motorized boat travel on Lake George that began in 1817. I wondered if the leaf peepers could see my bright windbreaker from the boat.

From the various angles, I could see how the color of the leaves differed. To the north, they were mostly dark maroon and yellow, while to the south there was still green mingling with the brilliant reds and oranges.

I had been up on Buck for about a half hour when a party of five hikers arrived; they had come from the other trail head. Shivering in the cold wind, they looked around and took some pictures, then quickly headed back down the mountain. Shortly thereafter, I did the same.

In a little over an hour, I was back at my car. During the drive home, on a whim, I got off the Northway at the Bolton exit and drove the short distance to Bolton Landing for a look at where I had just been. Buck Mountain, from the lake shore, stood out clearly to the east. I imagined there was now someone else up there admiring Lake George from the same vantage point I had just left.

To Get There

To get to the parking area I used, take Northway Exit 20 to Route 9. Follow Route 9 to Highway 149. Take 149 east for about five miles, then turn left on Buttermilk Falls Road; the Black Rooster Restaurant is at this intersection. Stay on Buttermilk Falls Road, which starts as hardtop and then becomes hard-packed dirt, until you come to a sign for the Lake George Trail System, 9.4 miles from Highway 149. There is a large parking area and sign-in register here.

The trail head you want is .5 mile beyond. To get there, drive down the road to the left that leads to another parking area. Here you will see signs to Buck Mountain Trail and other trails in the system.

To reach the more popular western trail head, take Highway 149 east to its intersection with Highway 9L. Drive seven miles north on 9L, then turn right where a sign indicates Kattskill Bay and Pilot Knob. It is 3.5 miles to the Pilot Knob and Buck Mountain trail head, which is on the right.

The western approach trail rises 1,990 feet in its 3.3-mile ascent; the eastern, 1,130 feet in its 2.3-mile climb.

Technical Information
Height: 2,334'
Trail length: 2.3 miles from the east
Difficulty: Moderate

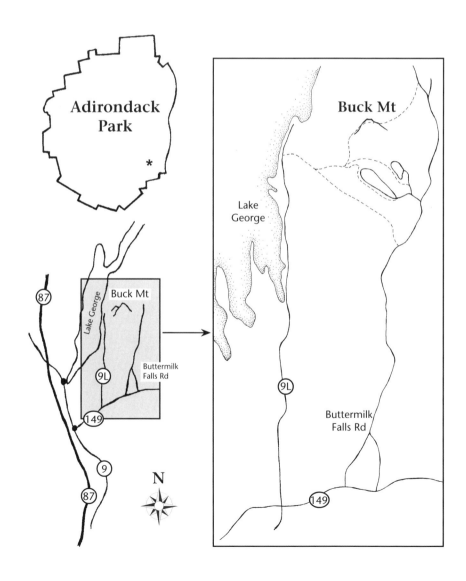

Top of Hadley offers 360-degree views. On a clear day, the Catskill high peaks can sometimes be seen in the distance.

As I looked due south from atop this not quite 2,700-foot Adirondack summit, I detected a mountain range far off in the distance. It was mid-June. The sky was hazy, the air filled with humidity, so I thought my eyes might be playing tricks on me. Later that day, back at the trail head, I looked at my maps and realized that I had, indeed, seen a mountain range—the Catskills! That was but one of the magnificent scenes that unfolded before my eyes on Hadley Mountain. By the time my daughter, Karalyn, and I finally completed our descent, we'd had many equally memorable and interesting experiences.

Our climb began at the parking area just off Tower Road. From the outset, the trail rose continuously for the first two-thirds of the way up the mountain, some of it over bare stone that looked like an old concrete road. The forest in this section was dominated by hardwoods such as oak, sugar maple and beech. Striped maple and other shrubs made up the understory. The ground was mostly covered with the previous fall's dead, dried leaves. It was in these leaves that we made our first interesting discovery.

Smooth rock outcroppings are frequently crossed on the Hadley Mountain climb.

For some reason, small creatures were on the move that day, their hopping making a mini-racket in the leaf matter. Karalyn went to investigate and brought back a small brownish toad—an American toad—and it wasn't alone. Along the climb we heard and saw about a hundred of these amphibians, who have toxin-producing glands (wart-like bumps) that protect them from most predators. Garter snakes, of which we saw a couple sunning themselves later on, have a resistance to this poison and prey heavily on these toads.

At about a mile and a quarter, the trail leveled off. That gave us a false sense of accomplishment, as in, "We finally made it!" But after a short distance, reality hit as we started to climb once again, finally coming out on an open area near the summit. The great views to the south were only a teaser; we still had to hike a short way past an abandoned DEC fire warden's cabin to reach the bare summit. It was then that the immensity of the terrain became apparent.

American toad

In the foreground to the south lay Great Sacandaga Lake, with the Mohawk Valley and the highest of the Catskill peaks off in the distance. To the northwest was Bearpaw and Mt. Blue and mountains beyond. To the north, the Adirondack High Peaks—Dix and Nippletop—could be seen against the horizon. But the viewing didn't stop there. To the northeast were mountains skirting the western shore of Lake Champlain, and farther down or almost directly east, the Green Mountains of Vermont.

Karalyn Aprill crossing the ridge just below the Hadley Mountain summit.

Even with this great vista spread out before us, there still was more to see. On Hadley's summit is a restored fire tower, a once-grim reminder of the forest fires that ravaged the area in the early 1900s. Now unused and restored by its sponsor, it waits for hikers to climb it for even more spectacular sights.

garter snake

In all, the two-mile hike with a vertical rise of 1,550 feet took us an hour. On the descent we took our time, since it can be difficult to put the brakes on in some of the steeper stretches. Hikers have to be careful to avoid the bare rocks in wet weather, as they can be slippery. In these stretches, the beaten path hugs one of the sides of the smooth bedrock.

In the parking area, ours was the only car, and we saw no one nor any signs of other people during the entire hike.

Hadley is a great climb, not only for its commanding views of the Adirondacks, but for the expansive vistas of the Mohawk Valley and Catskills to the south. Atop this small mountain, you feel as if you really can almost see forever.

To Get There

From the south, drive through Lake Luzerne Village on Stony Creek Road (Highway 1) roughly 3.5 miles, turning left on Hadley Hill Road. Take this road 3 miles to Riley Hill Road (also called Eddy Road). Take a right and drive one mile to where the dirt-covered Tower Road comes in on the left. The parking area is approximately 1.5 miles on the left.

From the north, take the Warrensburg exit and Highway 418 south. After crossing the Hudson, continue south on Warrensburg Road 8 miles, then take a sharp left on Hadley Road. It will take you to Riley Hill Road. Then follow directions above.

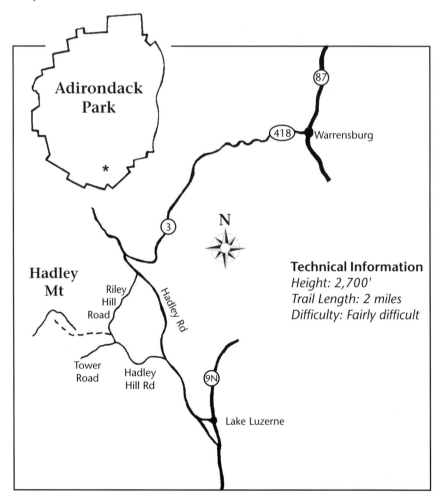

Adirondack Park

Warrensburg

N

Hadley Mt

Riley Hill Road

Hadley Rd

Tower Road

Hadley Hill Rd

Lake Luzerne

Technical Information
Height: 2,700'
Trail Length: 2 miles
Difficulty: Fairly difficult

Chapter 15

Author takes lunch break.

Cathead—what an unglamorous name for a little mountain that offers such terrific vistas from its summit! Maybe someone thought the mountain looked like a cat's head, though that is hard to imagine, or perhaps in the old days a mountain lion was shot in the head on the peak's bare top. Whatever the real story, I like to think Cathead got its name because it requires a few short, but focused, bursts of energy to reach its top, while the outstanding views sneak up on you as you approach the summit.

In late July, with the hawkweeks and wild daisies in flower, my daughter, Karalyn, and I drove down Benson Road just north of Great Sacandaga Lake to a trail head that begins in a parking area across from someone's house.

Cathead is different from other hikes described in this guide. Because the trail winds through sections of private property, hikers cannot venture far off the path, and dogs must be kept on a leash, which is the right thing to do on any trail.

hawkweed

Old power line set in large boulders is part of trail near the top of Cathead.

After crossing three small bridges, and hiking for about a half mile through a typical southern Adirondack forest of yellow birch, maple, beech and red oak, we began to climb steeply as the trail follows old power poles, once used to transport phone lines to a now abandoned fire warden cabin.

In this three-quarter-mile stretch to the top, it is a good idea to take frequent rest stops. Large boulders, part of a natural rock garden, make good seats. On the descent, consider taking the alternate dirt trail that hugs the side of the rock-strewn path.

grouse

Two thirds of the way up and after steady climbing, it happened! I had my head down, deep in thought, and Karalyn was seven or eight paces behind me, when all of a sudden all hell broke loose. Wings pounded as first a female ruffed grouse, then her half-dozen offspring, sprang up and blasted through the forest, branches breaking in their wake. To

Fire tower on Cathead is privately owned and is connected to a windmill that generates power.

make matters worse, the mother grouse then began her pathetic wounded-wing routine to lure us away from her little ones. If my heart had been working hard just in the climbing, this jolted it off the chart. After getting the old ticker back to semi-normal levels, I continued on, this time more alert and with Karalyn leading the way.

In another ten minutes we reached the abandoned cabin; after a short climb over a low ledge, we were at the summit, the landscape unfolding before us. The Silver Lake Wilderness, which includes some of the most remote areas in the Adirondack Park, spread out to our north and east.

To the south lay Great Sacandaga Lake and the Mohawk Valley beyond. The Catskill High Peaks on the horizon can be seen with field glasses on a clear day, as can the capital district of Albany.

The views were spectacular, but there was more to come. Cathead has a refurbished fire tower (privately owned) that can be climbed. From that vantage point, we got even better views to the north, which included Grant Lake below and Snowy Mountain off in the distance.

The only disconcerting note on the top of this 2,423-foot peak was the incessant clapping of a small windmill next to the tower. This windmill provides power for a relay on the tower. Another 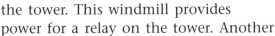 bizarre sight was the helicopter landing pad, a level area composed of stones covered with mesh, that juts from the side of the mountain. Helicopters apparently are used to service the electrical equipment on the summit, which is also private property but open to the public. This landing pad makes for another possible vantage point to view the landscape.

In all, the 2.8-mile round trip hike can easily be done in half a day. The day my daughter and I made the trek, we were the only people on Cathead, a small mountain that offered, for us, a lot more in the way of great views and excitement than its humble name implied.

To get there

From the south take the New York State Thruway west to Route 30 at Amsterdam. Take 30 north, eventually driving 3.2 miles past the intersection at the north end of Great Sacandaga Lake (don't turn right to Northville). Turn left on Benson Road. There is a yellow-on-brown DEC sign here that indicates the Northville-Lake Placid Trail. Drive 2.7 miles down Benson Road, then turn right on a newly paved road that leads to the trail head. There is a sign to Cathead at the turn.

From the north, take Northway Exit 26 (Pottersville) and then Route 9 south to Route 8. Follow Route 8 southwest until it meets Route 30. Take 30 south to the Benson Road turnoff and follow directions above.

Technical Information
Height: 2,423'
Trail length: 1.4 miles
Difficulty: Moderately difficult

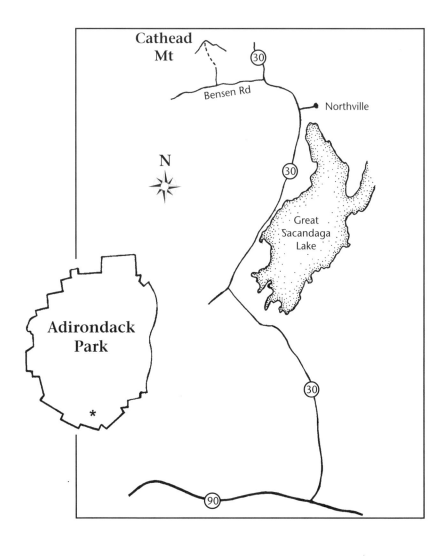

Chapter 16

Cloudy day from Kane Mountain.

When it comes to making a mountain out of a molehill, Kane Mountain in northern Fulton County fits the bill nicely. Rising only 2,200 feet above Canada and Pine lakes, Kane and its fire tower watch over a vast area of lakes and woods that includes the Silver Lake Wilderness to the north and the more settled Mohawk Valley to the south.

In early fall, my daughter, Karalyn, and I drove over to Caroga Lake and the Kane Mountain trail head just off Pine Lake Road to climb this small mountain. All along the three-hour drive, we had bright sunshine, as did most of northern New York. But when we came within 15 minutes of Caroga Lake, clouds and a low ceiling had settled in.

At the parking area a half mile off Route 10/29A north, there was just one other car. The trail head is marked by a yellow-on-brown DEC sign and is one of three trails leading up Kane. The hike starts with a gradual, easy ascent.

I love early fall hikes (the day after Labor Day is considered the unofficial beginning of fall in the Adirondacks) because the trails are generally quiet. The summer tourists are gone and the leaf peep-

The Kane Mountain firetower; it must be climbed six or seven flights for great views to the south.

ers haven't yet arrived. And in September the weather is often settled, with cool nights and sunny days. Trails are moist, and this moisture seems to release typical musty fall smells. Many of the migratory birds either are preparing to leave or have already gone, so there is a silence in the woods not experienced during the spring and summer. When you hear a squawk from a lingering bird, like a blue jay, you take notice as the screeching breaks the silence.

Kane was one of our easier mountain climbs; Karalyn and I walked gradually upward through a hardwood forest and reached the summit at .8 mile in about a half hour. Kane is the only mountain of the 23 low peaks in this book on which it is necessary to scale the fire tower for the views. It took us seven flights of stairs to clear the trees, and what unfolded before us was an impressive scene of clouds mixed with mountains, with Canada Lake below the only distinct landmark. On clear days, however, it is possible to see the Mohawk Valley south to the Catskills. We got this information from the woman who owned the other car in the parking lot; she joined us on the tower and told us she was a regular Kane climber.

blue jay

Abandoned fire warden cabin near tower.

As we gazed through the haze, I had a chance to review my notes on Adirondack fire towers, which were first constructed as wooden platforms in 1909. They were built in response to the large, destructive fires at the turn of the century. Fire wardens or watchers reported fires by telephone back then. Most of the watchers lived in cabins near the towers for a 22-week fire-watch period. Later on, the state replaced the wooden structures with the metal ones that still stand. At one time, 40 fire towers were in operation in the mountains; today, the state relies on aerial surveillance, mostly from private and commercial flights, to report forest fires.

As of this publication, Kane Mountain, which is on wild-forest-designated land, does not have a sponsor to restore the tower, but its steps are in fairly good condition.

After about an hour of puttering around, enjoying the early fall colors muted by the misty air, Karalyn and I headed down the gently sloping mountainside, spotting deer tracks along the way. Because of the forest type, this area is reported to hold large numbers of deer.

Although Kane is not one of the glamour-packed high peaks, this small mountain makes for a very pleasant, easy hike.

To get there

The most direct way to get to Kane Mountain from the south is to take the New York State Thruway west from Albany to Exit 28, then 30A north to Gloversville. At Gloversville, turn onto 29A and take it north to Caroga Lake. Three miles after the intersection of routes 10 and 29A, look for signs that point to Green Lake and Kane Mountain trail head on the right. The parking area is .5 miles down Green Lake Road.

From the north, take the Pottersville exit (26) from the Northway, then routes 9 and 8 to Route 30. Drive south on Route 30 to the Benson turnoff. Stay on this road until it ends at Route 125. Take 125 west to where it merges with Highway 112, continuing west to Route 10/29A. Then follow directions above.

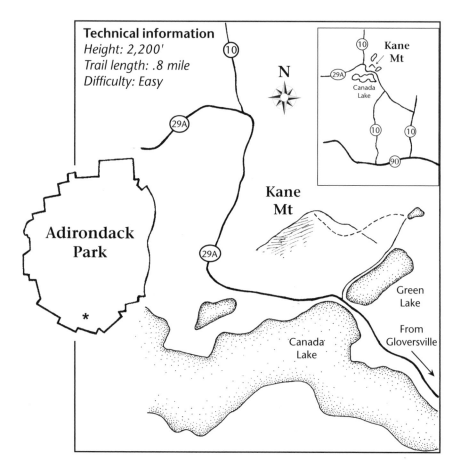

Technical information
Height: 2,200'
Trail length: .8 mile
Difficulty: Easy

N

Kane Mt

Adirondack Park

Kane Mt

29A

Canada Lake

Green Lake

From Gloversville

Chapter 17

Spectacle Lake as seen from Good Luck Mountain cliffs.

"Good luck," I said to myself, thinking I was being quite witty, since the mountain I was climbing was named Good Luck. My comment was made for encouragement, as my heart was pounding from the short, steep climb. However, when I finally did reach the summit and cliffs beyond and saw the panorama of Adirondack countryside before me, I fully believed the name Good Luck came from someone who realized the good fortune of his or her discovery.

I not only enjoyed the hard-earned great views from atop Good Luck Mountain, but later relaxed on a sandy beach on the nearby Good Luck Lake.

The trail head for both the mountain and the lake is off Route 10 in southern Hamilton County. From the well-marked parking area, I began hiking on a snowmobile trail, the direction shown by orange markers. Here, the walking was easy, and the trail wide as it wound through a young hardwood forest.

Red Spruce

Cave-like rock formation on trail up Good Luck.

At one-half mile, I came to a DEC sign-in registry; the trail then headed left. After about a mile, I caught my first glimpse of Good Luck Lake. The trail stays on higher ground as it follows the lake shore, but it is not difficult to bushwhack the short distance to the shoreline, as I did.

Back on the main trail, I continued on, crossing a small bridge and a knoll until I saw a second, more substantial bridge ahead. The unmarked path up Good Luck is on the right. When I was there, a large birch blocked the path, but the well-worn ground beyond was easy to spot.

The path up Good Luck Mountain has been described as everything from a goat trail to a bushwhack. I had no trouble following the worn path, however, first across a small brook and later as the trail rose abruptly 600 feet to the summit. In sections, orange and red plastic flagging tapes hung from branches, indicating the direction to take.

Good Luck cliffs offer a vantage point to view wild areas of the southwestern Adirondacks.

Next to the path lay huge boulders, some having fallen in such a way to appear to be caves. Throughout the climb, the partially visible cliffs, my ultimate destination, dominated the mountain's southern face and could be seen on my right.

Finally I reached the summit and the cliffs beyond. Spectacle Lake, looking appropriately like a pair of eyeglasses connected by a narrow strait, sat off in the distance with a maze of mountains and forests as its backdrop.

After catching my breath and admiring the scenery, I carefully climbed back down to the main trail for a side trip to a sandy beach on Good Luck Lake's western shore. This required a short hike that started at the bridge in the intersection and continued west. I found the beach to be a good place to cool off and rest before the return trip.

Having made the trip at mid-week, I had the beach all to myself, and when I returned to the parking area, mine was the only car there. All that, plus the great views from the mountain, made for "Good Luck."

To Get There

From Caroga Lake, drive north on 10/29A until 29A splits off to the left. Continue on 10 to the second bridge over the West Branch of the Sacandaga River, roughly five miles from the highway split. The well-marked parking area is on the left.

From Speculator, continue down Route 8 until Route 10 intersects. Drive south on Route 10, 12 miles to the parking area near the Sacandaga River bridge.

Technical Information
Height: 2,300 feet
Trail length: 2.5 miles
Difficulty: Moderate

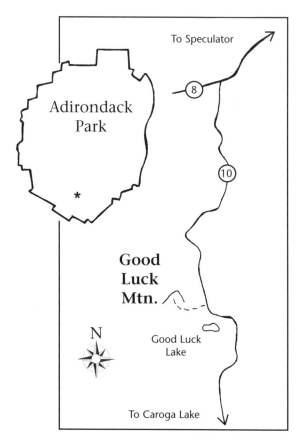

Chapter 18

Boulders and large hardwoods line path to Echo Cliffs.

Echo Cliffs—the name conjures up images of kids shouting from rocky precipices, their cries reverberating off mountains like stones skimming along the surface of a pond. I was anxious to try out my own bellowing and find out if I, too, could hear my echo when I stood atop those cliffs, which front Panther Mountain just west of Piseco Lake in Hamilton County.

The climb is a popular one, and in the spring and summer a number of cars are usually pulled off the side of the Old Piseco Road across from the trailhead, which is marked by a yellow-on-brown DEC sign.

The trail rises slightly at first, passing through a mature hardwood

Exposed roots indicate wear. The climb to Echo Cliffs is a short, popular one.

Beech showing old initials carved in bark.

forest dominated by beeches. These trees, with their smooth, easily cut bark, were at one time tempting targets for hikers who wanted to cut their initials or proofs of devotion into the large trunks. As I passed each beech tree, I didn't see any fresh carvings; perhaps young people today prefer instead to decorate their own bodies with tattoos and ornaments.

However, the artwork created by those woodcarvers of yesteryear is about to disappear, since many of these mature beeches are dying, a result of beech scale, a parasitic fungus. This hardwood forest, though, is still home to many typical spring flowers, such as trilliums.

Just before arriving at the cliffs and about a half mile into the hike, the trail gets steep. Here I had to do some fancy footwork using tree roots as crude stairs. After moving past some large rocks, I came out on top of the cliffs, which are 2,420 feet in elevation. Panther Mountain's summit, slightly northeast of where I stood, rises another 294 feet. It is wooded and provides no vistas, but the cliffs act as large viewing areas.

trillium

Higgins Bay of Piseco Lake sat below, with the Silver Lake Wilderness beyond. Near where I stood, a woman was taking in the sun, sound asleep on a slab of stone. Her grandchildren were running about on the rocks. I waited for her to wake up before trying the experiment I had planned: shouting, then waiting to hear if I would, indeed, hear an echo.

Woman naps atop Echo Cliffs as her grandson runs toward her. Piseco Lake is in the background.

While I waited, I thought of the Greek myth in which a young nymph named Echo was punished by Hera, the queen of the gods, who believed the beautiful young woman was in love with her husband, Zeus. Echo's punishment was that she could never again initiate a conversation, but only repeat what was said to her.

As soon as the resting woman woke up, I gave a few loud calls but heard no echo. Maybe it was because of the weather conditions that day, or possibly the person who named the cliffs had a romantic imagination.

After a half hour taking pictures, I headed down to the trail head along the well-worn trail. On the way, I met hikers coming up, among them a camp group with two adults and ten kids. The Panther Mountain-Echo Cliffs trek is a good one for families with young children because the climb is short and only steep at the very end.

As that group passed by, talking loudly, I wondered if, after I reached the road, I might hear their shouting from atop the cliffs and perhaps their echoes, too. I waited at the trail head for awhile, but heard nothing. Perhaps, in fact, it was a hopeless romantic who named them Echo Cliffs.

To get there

From the north, take the Northway to the Pottersville exit (26), then Route 9 south to Route 8. Stay on Route 8 past Speculator and Ox Bow Lake (8.7 miles from the junction of Routes 8 and 30 in Speculator). Turn right on the Old Piseco Road and follow it 5.3 miles, where you will see a yellow-on-brown DEC sign marking the Panther Mountain-Echo Cliffs trail.

From the south, take Route 10 north to the intersection with Route 8 just before Piseco Lake. Turn right; look for the Old Piseco Road sign a little over three miles on the left.

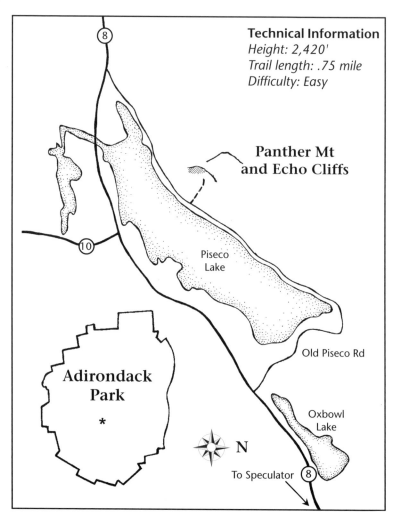

Technical Information
Height: 2,420'
Trail length: .75 mile
Difficulty: Easy

Panther Mt and Echo Cliffs

Piseco Lake

Old Piseco Rd

Adirondack Park

Oxbowl Lake

N

To Speculator

The Fulton Chain of Lakes, mist rising above the warm water after a cold night, as seen from Bald Mountain.

When you climb Bald Mountain, which rises between Old Forge and Inlet, you move up a trail that gives you almost instant gratification in the form of glimpses off to the left of the Fulton Chain of Lakes.

As you ascend even farther, you become more concerned with the immediate scenery. Staying on the path is paramount, especially when you emerge on a sheer rock spine that makes you imagine mounting the back of a triceratops from the Cretaceous Period. In fact, this rock was already very old, up to a billion years old, when triceratops roamed the earth.

triceratops

When you finally reach the narrow summit at 2,350 feet, you come upon a fire tower that stands starkly, straddling the Precambrian rock. But as

Bald Mountain trail includes a section of sheer rock arched at a 90-degree angle.

you approach the tower and look off in the distance, you quickly rejoin the 20th century when you see boats of all shapes moored on First Lake and the faint outlines of buildings on the shoreline.

I climbed Bald Mountain in early August in the middle of the week, arriving at the trail head about 9 a.m.* My expectations for getting great views with little hiking effort were realized. The trail head to this low peak is 4.5 miles north of the Visitor Center in Old Forge. To get there, I took a left off Route 28 onto Rondaxe Road and pulled into the parking area, .1 miles down on the left.

The climb up Bald Mountain starts almost at once, rising through a hardwood forest of maples, birch, and some beech. There was still some blowdown near the trail, a reminder of the big windstorm that had blown through the region two summers before. As I moved upward, I tried to follow the beaten path. When that disappeared, I stayed close to the cliffs that continue to the top. It was near these cliffs that the path once again reappeared.

As altitude increases, some hardwoods are replaced by softwoods such as spruce and balsam. Just before the summit, I came upon what seemed to be the remains of a building with only the roof left lying on the ground. Maybe this had been a shelter for those who made the climb in winter.

On the final approach to the top, I had to jump from boulder to boulder in places and then return to the sheer rock spine until I reached the tower at the summit. It was worth the effort because the views that morning, with mist rising off the lakes below, were magnificent. Directly ahead to the southeast sat First Lake with the

---

*Readers should know that while Bald Mountain receives more traffic than other climbs in this book, the views make it worthwhile and you can avoid too much company by choosing your time carefully.

narrows leading into the expanse of Fourth Lake to the northeast. Only one boat traveling north disturbed the mirror-like surface. Due east, off in the distance, was the outline of Wakely Mountain, with Blue Mountain cutting the horizon on its left.

What a perfect vantage point to observe the Fulton Chain, I thought. Mine was not an original observation, for it has been written that a century and a half earlier, the famous North Country hunter and trapper Nat Foster used to climb up to this open mountain top and use it as a lookout spot. Foster is believed to be one of the models for James Fenimore Cooper's fictional character, Natty Bumppo. Like Bumppo, also called

Bald Mountain tower straddles narrow, bare, rock-faced summit.

Hawkeye, Foster was known to be an expert shot.

Unlike Foster, though, I had the advantage of climbing the refurbished fire tower for an even better vantage, one that opened vistas of more mountains to the north and west. After an hour of exploring, I headed down to the parking area, passing some early morning hikers on their way up. They asked for information. I told them about the trail conditions and the distance they had to go, but that was all. I decided to let them discover for themselves the great views they would find from atop that ancient mass of rock.

To get there

There are a number of ways to get to Old Forge. The easiest from the south is to take the New York State Thruway west to Utica, then take Route 28 north.

From the north, take Route 30 to 28N/30 at Long Lake, then 28 south to Inlet. Rondaxe Road is roughly 5 miles south of the village.

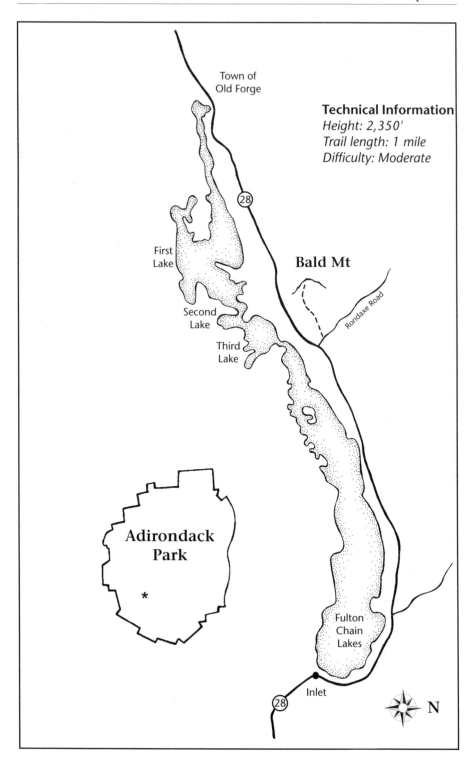

Town of
Old Forge

Technical Information
Height: 2,350'
Trail length: 1 mile
Difficulty: Moderate

28

First
Lake

Bald Mt

Second
Lake

Rondaxe Road

Third
Lake

**Adirondack
Park**

*

Fulton
Chain
Lakes

28   Inlet

N

Grasses sprout from the soil wedged between bare rocks on Black Bear Mountain summit. The mountaintop burned decades ago and vegetation is just starting to grow back.

As I surveyed the wild valleys and wetlands below the mostly open summit of Black Bear Mountain, I thought about how, by chance, I had learned about this relatively remote peak earlier that day.

I had just climbed Bald Mountain and had planned to stop and climb Rocky Mountain—a short, easy ascent—on my way home. While on Bald, I met a woman climber who knew the southwestern Adirondacks well. I told her of my plans. Her reply was immediate: "Don't climb Rocky if you want peace and quiet; it is a very popular climb. Try Black Bear instead. It's a longer walk and a little steep toward the end, but you won't meet up with the crowds."

As I sat atop Black Bear, I realized she was right. The only thing that disturbed my peace was a sonic blast from a military jet doing maneuvers overhead. It created a boom that echoed throughout the valley, and this single, disconcerting noise only accentuated the remoteness of Black Bear.

Trail marker to Black Bear Mountain. There are two paths up Black Bear; the author chose the more direct trail on the right.

To get to the trail head, I pulled in at the parking area .9 mile south of the village of Inlet. There are actually two trail heads here. The one on the left, with a DEC marker, goes to Rocky; the one on the right, which is unmarked, leads to Black Bear. As I watched two carloads of people heading up Rocky, I took the path less traveled to Black Bear.

After a short rise, the trail levels off until it reaches an intersection with a sign pointing to Black Bear, 2.1 miles to the right. Beyond the intersection is a clearing, then a short rise where hardwoods mix with softwoods like hemlock, spruce, and balsam. The trail has its share of wet spots; Gore-Tex-lined hiking boots are almost a must for this trip. Early on, the walk was quite level on what appeared to be a path that serves as a winter cross-country ski trail.

Near one wet area, I looked down and saw, very appropriately, a black bear track about the size of my fist. There are an estimated 3,500 of these omnivores in the Adirondacks. They are powerfully built, but there is really nothing to fear if you

black bear

Bear claw marks on beech tree.

meet up with one on the trail. Just follow a few common-sense rules: don't offer food; don't get between a mother and her cubs; and don't run away, even if the bear doesn't move.

Black bears have poor eyesight, but excellent hearing. Sometimes it takes a little while for the bear to recognize you as a human. For example, on one hike a couple of years ago, I met up with a large bear who began crossing the trail in front of me, then stopped and faced me. The wind was blowing hard, so I figured he hadn't heard me, and since I stood completely still, he was having a hard time figuring out what I was. After a few moments, I called out a few commands like "Get moving," which it did. Had it not moved along, I would have backed away slowly, facing it, and waited until it moved on, or maybe made a detour away from it.

Unlike bears in the more heavily used High Peaks region, where some come in contact with humans on a regular basis and become bold, bears on the less-traveled trails described in this book are more apt to take off at the first sign of a human. So consider it good fortune if you see a bear on your climb.

The final short ascent of Black Bear Mountain is a difficult one. It requires a little rock scaling and climbing while holding on to tree roots. This could be a tough stretch for young children or more elderly hikers.

Finally, I reached the mostly open summit, the site of a fire many decades ago. I was alone. The bare rock on the summit was home to mosses and reindeer lichen, mountain ash, grasses, and some smaller spruce and balsam. By walking around the summit, I was treated to a number of different views, each with its own perspective. At one spot, Raquette Lake could be seen ahead with the Santanoni Range beyond. A little to the east were Blue Mountain and Wakely Mountain, with Seventh Lake to the south.

On my way down, I met up with a group of climbers that included a couple with younger children. Another mile farther on, a grandmother and her granddaughter rested on downed logs. "Is it this easy all the way?" she asked. "Not really," I answered. "You may be in for a couple of difficult places by the time you reach the top, but once you get there, you'll see it was all worth it."

To get there

From the south take Route 28 1.2 miles north of Eagle Bay to the well-marked parking area on the left. From the north, the parking area is .9 mile south of Inlet on the right.

Technical information
Height: 2,448'
Trail length: 2.1 miles
Difficulty: Easy at first, final ascent difficult

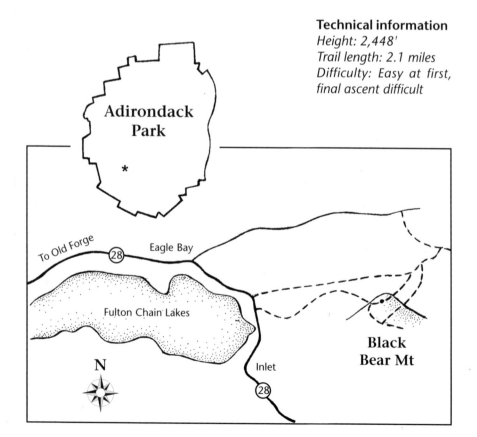

Cranberry Lake with Joe Indian Island in the distance as seen from the lookout spot on Bear Mountain.

As I gazed down at Cranberry Lake from the clear overlook on the west side of Bear Mountain, I wondered if timber wolves, during their waning years in the Adirondacks a century earlier, had gathered here to howl on moonlit August nights. The Cranberry Lake area is said to be the place where these large predators made their last stand in New York State.

While I continued to gaze out over the beautiful lake, past Joe Indian Island and the low hills beyond, I heard, instead of the eerie howl of a a wolf, the drone of a seaplane taking off from a dock at Cranberry Lake Village off to my right.

My 13-year-old son, Colin, and I had just hiked the 1.7-mile trail that begins inside the DEC campgrounds. It was late August, and there was already some color in the sugar maple leaves.

sugar maple

Along the relatively easy climb from the campground, we first hiked through stands

This picture was taken in Canada and depicts a pack of wolves, Canis lupus Lycaon, *the small wolf that used to inhabit the Adirondacks. Bogs like the one pictured are common in the Cranberry Lake area.*

dominated by old-growth yellow birch, a tree that can live for 200 or more years, and equally ancient hemlocks. Some say the latter's top branches always point east, so this tree can be used as an emergency direction finder. I've never been so badly lost that I've had to prove or disprove this theory.

At .8 mile, we reached a DEC lean-to, which was unoccupied, and .4 mile farther on a steeper ascent we came to Bear's wooded summit. The overlook was another .4 mile along the mountain crest. Although the scenic overlook provides a limited view, it is an impressive one of lake, islands, and hills.

While Colin devoured snacks, my mind wandered back to the original Adirondack wolves, whose scientific name is *Canis lupus Lycaon*. This subspecies still roams parts of southern Ontario and Quebec, and there have been a number of reported wolf sightings in the Adirondacks in recent years. I even spotted one myself.

With the current debate over restoring wolves to these mountains, assuming they're not already here, it is worth taking a look at some of their physical and biological characteristics. *Lycaon* is a very

Along the trail, Colin Aprill stops for a rest.

small wolf, with males averaging 65 pounds and females 53 pounds. They hunt in packs of about six family members.

After the wolf pups are born in their den in the spring, the mature wolves bring them food. By August, these growing youngsters can travel with the pack, and they move to an open area such as a spruce bog or perhaps even an overlook on a lake shore like the one where I stood. While the adults hunt, the adolescents remain in the rendezvous site and communicate with their parents by howling. *Lycaon*'s principal food sources are beaver in summer and white-tailed deer in winter. Because of their small stature, *Lycaon* cannot bring down a healthy adult moose, but they will eat road-killed and weakened moose.

When Colin finished his snack, we headed back to the campsite. We had two options. We could continue straight ahead past the overlook, winding our way down the other side of the mountain to the campsite road, or we could backtrack. We chose the latter.

On the way down, I paid more attention to our tracks and the imprints made by animals the night before, when it had rained. I saw deer tracks in places and one set of coyote tracks. This coyote, *Canis latrans*, was one of thousands whose ancestors migrated to New York State from southern Canada during the 1930's, first colonizing, then filling the niche left by the timber wolf. Also called brush wolves, eastern coyotes can be heard howling on still nights in mid-August along the shores of Cranberry Lake.

coyote

To get there

From the east and west, take Route 3 to the marked campsite road just east of the hamlet of Cranberry Lake. It is a 1.3-mile drive to the campground, where you must pay a $5.00 day-use fee. The trail head and parking area are .4 mile inside the campground on the left side of the road.

Technical information
Height: 2,520'
Trail length: 1.6 miles
Difficulty: Moderate

* Adirondack Park

Silver Lake

Cranberry Lake

3

3

Bear Mt

Campground

Cranberry Lake

N

View from Mt. Frederika looking southeast to Lake Lila with Shingle Shanty Brook in the distance.

Deer tracks dot its trail; ravens, an osprey, and an eagle fly above it; the occasional moose passes through—this is the Lake Lila Primitive Area (now classified Wilderness), in central Hamilton County in the heart of the Adirondacks. The streams in this Wilderness Area—a 7,215-acre block—flow into two major watersheds: the Beaver River flowing west and the Raquette flowing north. It was to this remote area that I traveled in early July to climb Mt. Frederika for a better view of this wild place.

Just getting to Lake Lila is an adventure that starts south of Tupper Lake where I turned west on Route 10A, the Circle Road (there is a sign pointing toward Sabattis, another to the William C. Whitney Area) and drove 3 miles to the shore of Little Tupper Lake, the eastern point of a recent, well-publicized state land acquisition. From here I traveled west on Route 10, past the former Whitney Headquarters, now a state ranger base, to a sign on the left pointing the direction to the Lake Lila parking area 5.6 miles farther on. This is a very narrow dirt road that requires slow driving. At one point, I had

Loon swimming on Lake Lila.

to wait for a doe to cross the road before moving on. The land bordering the access road is private.

At the parking area I had two options. If I had brought along a canoe, I could have portaged the .3 mile to the boat launch and paddled 3 miles to a lean-to at the western end of the lake to begin my climb. Instead, I chose to walk the entire way, a 4.5-mile hike.

The first third of the hike, through mixed hardwood forest interspersed with the occasional wetland, is on a relatively flat, well-maintained DEC access road. Even after the heavy rains of earlier that week, this road was primarily dry, making for firm walking.

At 1.5 miles, I got my first glimpse of Lake Lila and followed a narrow side trail a short distance to a small campsite near a sandy beach. From here I could see the cliffs of Mt. Frederika, my destination, off in the distance. At one point, a raging 20-foot wide Harrington Brook cascaded down a rock-filled bed and passed under the road on its way to the lake a short distance away.

I continued west, the trail skirting the lakeshore. In a quiet reedy bay, a loon floated undisturbed. I photographed it and moved on, coming to a lean-to at 3 miles. Here I met the only person I would see in the Primitive Area that day. We chatted and he told me his

brother-in-law, who was out on the lake fishing, had caught some lake trout. Lake Lila
also holds brook trout, smallmouth bass
and landlocked salmon (stocked).

From the lean-to (a logical place
for canoeists to leave for the
climb), the still hard-packed
road/trail passes near two interesting historical sites—Nehasane Lodge Site and the old
Remson-Lake Placid Railroad
Bed. The Nehasane (also

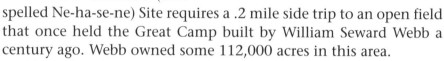

spelled Ne-ha-se-ne) Site requires a .2 mile side trip to an open field
that once held the Great Camp built by William Seward Webb a
century ago. Webb owned some 112,000 acres in this area.

The railroad, built by Webb, has not been in use since 1980 and
is now a public snowmobile corridor trail. I crossed it a short time
later as the road rose gradually. After one mile, I saw the sign to the
summit of Mt. Frederika, .5 mile to the right. The road, going straight
ahead, ends at Partlow Pond.

The very narrow, somewhat wet trail up Mt. Frederika is not a
difficult climb, though there are slippery spots where it crosses bare
rock. Signs of the big blowdown, the microburst of July 15, 1995,
are visible with large trees uprooted on both sides of the path. Re-
generation is evident in the form of young saplings pushing upward and mixing with larger unscathed trees.

Beyond the summit, I came out on the cliffs and got a breathtaking view of Lake Lila sparkling below. There was not a boat or
canoe in sight. I sat down on a patch of flat rock to admire the
scene. Blue Mountain sat straight ahead in the distance, the Santanoni range to the north. At the far end of Lake Lila was an open
bog-like area near where Shingle Shanty Brook enters the lake. As I
was surveying the landscape, a raven "cr-ruked" from somewhere
to my left.

I tried to imagine how the original owner, William Seward Webb,
could possibly have had enough money to own all this land, and
gain the luxury of naming these lakes and mountains after his family and friends. At one time he had 9,000 acres fenced off; then he
stocked in the enclosure animals like moose and elk, extirpated

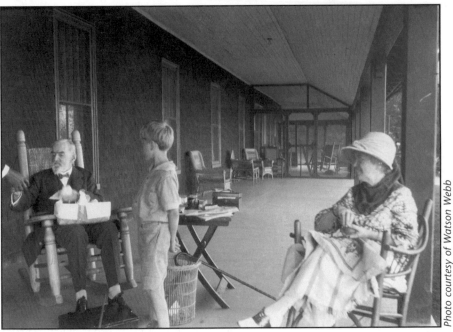

Photo courtesy of Watson Webb

William Seward Webb and his grandson Watson Webb at Nehasene Lodge, 1927.

from New York at that time. The whole idea of all this was mind boggling. After an hour of reflection and observation, I left.

On my return, I took the short side trip to the Nehasane Lodge Site. The original lodge is described by one historian this way:

"The long, low building, gabled, and rimmed by verandas where guests might rock away the evening or dream in a hammock was in keeping with an age when luxurious camps were commonplace. Eight chimneys surmounted the whole. A striped awning, raised to shade one of the porches, relieved the somber shingled facade, while flower beds and a manicured lawn rambled through curving drives to the shore."

The writer goes on to describe the interior with its posh elegance mixing with the usual great camp ornaments: an assortment of stuffed animals, birds and fish.

The lodge was taken down by the state in the late 1970s. The area is now an open meadow that serves as a large campground. Beyond the lodge site, the Beaver River exits Lila on its way to Stillwater Reservoir and eventually the Black River and Lake Ontario.

The hike back was uneventful. Though there were now 10 cars in the parking area and it was the day before the big Independence Day weekend, I had only met up with that one camper at the lean-to. The solitude was befitting this beautiful out-of-the-way, area.

Trip Tips

There are designated campsites scattered along the shores of Lake Lila, and generally those beyond the lean-to on the west side are less heavily used. Camping is allowed on four of the seven islands (one party per island), but these are very popular spots and finding an open campsite on a weekend may be difficult.

Traveling by canoe to a campsite, then hiking up Mt. Frederika, is a good option. A .3-mile trail goes from the parking area to the lake. No outboard motors are allowed.

Overnight accommodations are available in Long Lake and Tupper Lake villages. For a listing of motels and bed and breakfasts, contact the Tupper Lake Chamber of Commerce at (518) 359-3328.

An interesting side trip, especially for those with canoes, is to drive east to the William C. Whitney Area Ranger Station (formerly Whitney Headquarters) about 9 miles from Lake Lila. The parking area is below the station where there is a boat launch (no outboards). The Whitney Area became state land on June 1, 1999. It is classified Wilderness.

To Get There

From Long Lake, drive about 7 miles north on Route 30. The Circle Road/Route 10A sign to Sabattis is on the left. (DEC sign to Whitney Wilderness Area is also on the left.) Take the Circle Road past Little Tupper Lake and the state ranger station (formerly Whitney Headquarters) about 8 miles to a sign pointing left to the Lake Lila parking area 5.6 miles farther on. This is a narrow dirt road, and slow, careful driving is a must.

Land on both sides of this road is private and no parking is allowed. The state parking lot holds 30 cars (no trailers allowed). If it is full, you must drive back to the Sabattis Road and park, then walk the 5.6 miles to the trail head.

Technical Information
Height: 2,200 feet
Trail Length: 4.75 miles
Difficulty: Moderately easy, but long

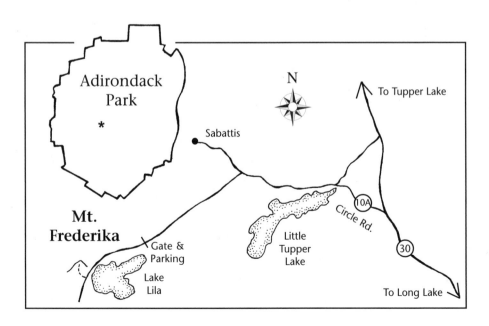

Chapter 23

Fog-shrouded view from Mt. Arab, looking south toward Eagle Crag Pond.

Mt. Arab rises just west of Tupper Lake; the firetower atop this 2,545-foot peak once guarded huge tracts of wilderness—some of the most remote sections of the Adirondacks — from forest fires.

On a Saturday morning in mid-March, I drove west of Tupper just across the St. Lawrence County line to climb this small mountain. The parking area, a pullover off the Mt. Arab Road that dead-ends three miles farther on, is opposite the marked trail head.

As I began the ascent through a young hardwood forest, I knew my timing was right. The cold night had left a crust of snow so hard that it rivaled a city sidewalk. I carried along snowshoes with crampons anyway, just in case there were some icy sections up ahead.

The one-mile trail up Mt. Arab climbs modestly, then levels before rising again, giving me time to catch my breath. After a couple of hundred yards, I crossed an old deer track frozen in the crust. That would be the only deer track I would see. As I continued my upward journey, the snow thinned and, in places facing the south,

Fire tower atop Mt. Arab.

disappeared entirely. On the northern slope, the icy snow was at least a foot deep.

About two-thirds of the way up Mt. Arab, the trail follows a ridge, climbs over some ledges which were ice covered, then rises again until it comes out at the open summit. Although a major snow and ice storm was predicted for later that day and there was some cloud cover hiding distant peaks, I could see Piercefield Flow of the Raquette River to the north. Ahead was the firetower and a framed-out cabin soon to become an interpretative center.

I climbed the tower and looking south saw what appeared to be Eagle Crag Lake; to the west, off in the distance melding with the overcast horizon, were the forests of the Five Ponds Wilderness, one of the more remote areas in the Adirondacks. To the east, I could see Tupper Lake, partially hidden by a mountain in the foreground.

The firetower and cabin were built in 1918, and replaced a wooden tower constructed in 1912. It is now the only one of seven towers erected in St. Lawrence County that is still standing. Currently, the Friends of Mt. Arab (P.O. Box 185, Piercefield, NY 12973) are raising money to complete the restoration project.

After taking in the scenery, doing some photography and relaxing, I headed down the trail, finding the trip down on the hard-

Fire-warden's cabin atop Mt. Arab is being restored and will become an interpretive center.

packed snow and ice tougher than going up. At times I took to the undisturbed crust that bordered the path, instead of trying to walk on ice.

At the parking area, I put my pack in my truck and drove back toward Tupper Lake. A short distance from the trail head, I crossed the old railroad tracks that run from Utica to Lake Placid. I remember a friend from Tupper Lake, Frank Morrison, correcting me when I told him of my plan to climb Mt. Arab. "It's Aaaarab," he said. "That's the way the conductors announced the stop in the old days, Mt. Aaaarab." However you pronounce it, Mt. Arab made for a nice late winter climb.

To Get There

To get to the trail head/parking area from Tupper Lake Village, take Route 3 to Piercefield. At 2.3 miles beyond the sign markeing the St. Lawrence County line, turn left onto the Conifer Road, go 1.7 miles, then turn left again onto the Mt. Arab Road (there is a sign pointing the way) .8 mile to where the marked trail starts on the left.

Technical Information
Height: 2,545
Trail length: 1 mile
Difficulty: Moderate

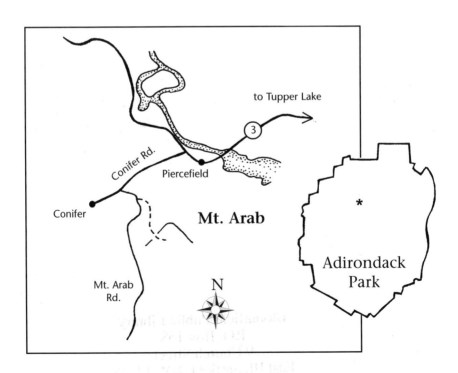

The St. Regis area as seen from the Azure summit with ponds, lakes, and thick forest in foreground, making the trip to the Azure trail head an adventure.

Azure is the most northerly mountain described in this book and it may very well be the most remote. Just getting to the trail head can be an adventure, but the short climb and the accompanying scene of the St. Regis Canoe Area and other equally wild country easily makes up for the long ride.

The trail head for Azure is located off Blue Mountain Road in the town of Santa Clara, in Franklin County. There are two ways to reach this point. From the north, take Route 458 west of its intersection with Route 30. Travel on 458 two miles or so past the small village of Santa Clara until you come to a left turn at Blue Mountain Road. The trail head is seven miles south; a metal building partially hidden in the woods on the left is opposite the parking area.

A second and even more adventurous way to get to this parking area is to take Keese Mill Road, which begins off Route 30 just after the Paul Smith's College gym. The first eight miles are on increas-

Fire tower on Azure surrounded by stunted vegetation. Author is in front of fire tower.

ingly deteriorating hardtop that finally melds into dirt for the final nine miles. Don't take this option during mud season (usually in April or May). This is wild, uninhabited country with little through traffic, so you might have to wait quite awhile if you get stuck.

I climbed Azure in August, first coming in from the north, then returning by Keese Mill Road for variety. Once my son, Colin, and I got settled at the trail head, we began to focus on the one-mile climb.

We hiked past a gate and followed a marked trail a short distance to an old ranger station. Just after this building, the ascent began. Though short, it is a fairly steep climb through a hardwood forest of maple, white and yellow birch, and white ash.

During this steep climb we kept telling ourselves that it wasn't far to the top, and took plenty of rest stops. Finally, the trail leveled out, weaving through slash and brambles and ending on an open summit. Pin and choke cherries are among the dominant shrubs here. Set in the clearing is an old fire tower with the lower steps removed to prevent climbing. The remaining steps appeared unsafe, so we enjoyed the scenery from the mountain summit.

Moose are becoming more plentiful in the Azure Mountain area of northern Franklin County.

Impressive views of the St. Regis Canoe Area and the High Peaks off in the distance framed the nearby countryside--a mix of softwood forest, bogs, and ponds that gave us a real feel for the mountain's remoteness. It reminded me of the fact that some of the first moose that repopulated New York in 1980 chose this very same county to make their home. The town of Santa Clara held an estimated three moose at a time when there were only five or so in the entire state. One cow moose was seen regularly along Red Tavern Road, just north of Azure.

Today, there are an estimated 60 to 75 moose in the state, most residing in the Adirondacks. Two key sites where they are reproducing are in the Moose River Plains of Hamilton County and the Azure Mountain area of Franklin County. It is these key regions that will provide moose to repopulate the rest of the mountains.

After an hour of relaxing and enjoying the remoteness (we were the only people on the mountain that day), Colin and I took it easy on the way down. From the trail head we returned home via Blue Mountain Road, which gradually blends into Keese Mill Road. In places, these roads parallel the St. Regis River.

To get there

From the north, take Blue Ridge Road two miles west of Santa Clara on Route 458. Go south seven miles to the trail head on the right.

From the south take Keese Mill Road 17 miles to the trail head on the left. A metal building in the woods is opposite the parking area.

Technical information
Height: 2,518'
Trail length: 1 mile
Difficulty: Moderate

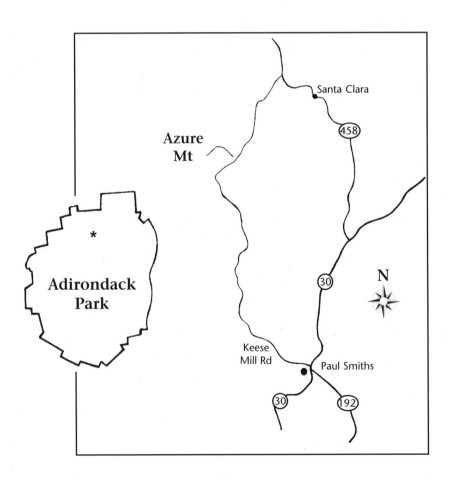

Chapter 25

Looking north from top of Jenkins.

The trail up Jenkins Mountain is unique in a couple of ways. First, it is a relatively new trail, cut in the early 1990s, and second, Jenkins was the first mountain in the Adirondacks for which climbers needed a permit. The permit system was abandoned in 1996 because the 8.2-mile round-trip hike didn't attract the hordes of climbers that had been expected. It is still not heavily used, and the hiker can enjoy a peaceful climb and great views of the rugged, wild country north of Paul Smiths.

The hike up Jenkins begins at the Paul Smiths Visitor Interpretive Center (VIC) on Route 30, a half mile north of Paul Smith's College. A trail map is available at the VIC.

I climbed Jenkins in mid-October, not long after the new trail had opened to the public. Many of the leaves had gone by, but there were still some bright yellows mixed with the deep maroons and greens of the softwoods. The trail begins at a gazebo near the parking area. Blue trail markers indicate the short distance to where the path shifts to the left and follows Old Jenkins Mountain Road.

esker

For the next two miles, the hiking was easy along this old road-way, the ruts covered with leaf matter. At two miles, the trail narrows, and on that trip I needed to maneuver around a flooded section of road. The beaver dam on my left made for a dry, though shaky, detour.

The road soon gives way to a forest trail that rises to the top of a narrow esker. Red maples are the predominant tree in the area, with some growing to sizable proportions on the esker. This is unusual because most eskers, with their sandy soil, are home to pines.

Eskers are composed of glacial outwash deposited by a stream formed under a retreating glacier. They are made up of sand and stones that are usually stratified into distinct layers. For example, one layer may be almost entirely stones, while the one above it is sand or gravel.

After about three miles, the trail turns abruptly to the right and begins to gradually ascend through a mixed hardwood forest. This area on the backside of the mountain burned in 1903, and has since been reforested with maples and other northern hardwoods. The fall day that I climbed, the strong scent of earth and fallen leaves permeated the air.

Group of hikers from Germany at start of Jenkins Mountain trail.

Finally, the steep ascent to the summit began. At four miles, I turned left for the final .1–mile walk to the bare rock outcropping at the summit. Although the peak fall foliage was past, the scenery was still colorful with muted reds and yellows mingling with various shades of green bogs and softwood forests. I saw St. Regis Mountain in the foreground, and much farther to the north, Azure Mountain.

On my trip down the mountain, I met the only other group hiking the trail that day; they were from Germany.

At 8.2 miles, the Jenkins climb is the longest described in this book, but most of the trail is on relatively flat old roads. Allow five hours for the round trip.

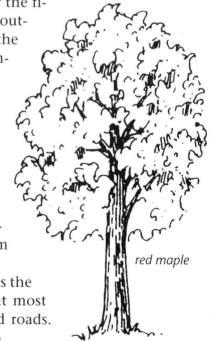

red maple

To get there

Drive .5 mile north of the intersection of routes 30 and 86 at Paul Smiths to the Visitors Interpretive Center (VIC). A great blue heron sign is at the turnoff. Park and pick up a map at the VIC.

Technical information
Height: 2,514'
Trail length: 4.1 miles
Difficulty: Moderate

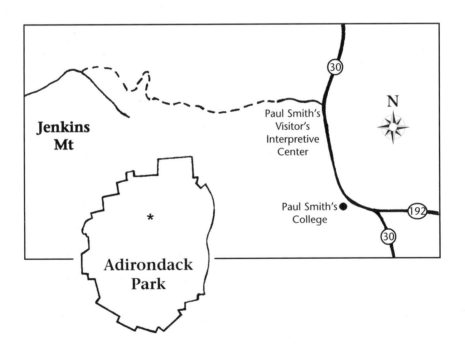

Chapter 26

Silver Lake spreads out below mountain of same name.

The sheer size and length of the cliffs that make up the south face of Silver Lake Mountain are impressive; they are easily seen from a distance. But what makes the Silver Lake Mountain climb distinctive for me are the trees: tall, straight red pines are dominant on this small mountain which, though only 2,378 feet high, provides great views from its open summit.

The well-marked trail head lies off Silver Lake Road, one mile southeast of Silver Lake. The climb starts immediately through a group of hardwoods, then the trail levels off as it crosses a small knoll.

When I made this climb in the fall, I was accompanied by my wife and two children. We encountered no other hikers on either the ascent or descent, probably because it was midweek and rain was in the offing.

About a third of a mile up, we emerged onto a rock outcrop. Some of the hardwoods had dropped their leaves, opening the canopy and allowing us a glimpse of Taylor Pond in the distance. After

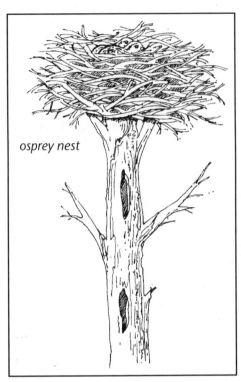

osprey nest

some level walking, we came to a forest dominated by red pines. Then the trail took an abrupt right and began a steady climb to the summit. Red pines continued to border the trail as it rose.

This section of the hike is my favorite; I love being enveloped by these beautiful softwoods with their rough reddish-brown bark. Their fallen needles cushion each stride. In the fall, they give off the strong, aromatic scent of pine.

The trail narrows as it approaches the summit and comes close to the cliffs. This is a good place to keep small children close at hand, as the pine needles, especially when wet, can be slippery.

When we reached the summit, it began to drizzle, then to rain steadily, but we were prepared and donned our rain gear. The moisture seemed to impart a richness to the peak fall colors, especially the reds and oranges of the maples. The yellows of the poplar and birch looked deeper, since the color was not washed out by a bright sun.

Below us, over the little knob we had climbed earlier, a small, thin cloud hovered, gyrating like a snake slithering across a branch. Ahead we saw Taylor Pond with Silver Lake to the right and Union Falls Pond off in the distance. Catamount and Whiteface framed the horizon, but it was the small pond just below the cliffs that really stood out; jutting out of its waters was an osprey nest set in a tall dead tree.

The cliffs beneath us stretch for miles until they meld into Potter Mountain to the east. These cliffs were the site of one of the first peregrine falcon restoration projects in the early 1980s. From 1981 to 1984 dozens of peregrines were raised on nesting ledges by the Department of Environmental Conservation biologists. One pair

Red pine grips rock summit of Silver Lake Mountain.

of released falcons returned in 1987, but the DEC, according to Barbara Loucks of the Endangered Species Unit, has found no new nests since then. Loucks asks climbers to contact the DEC if they see any peregrines in the area.

Peregrine falcons are dark on top with a white-barred underside. They are 15 to 20 inches long, weigh about two pounds, and have a wingspan of around 40 inches. Their wings, when opened, are more angular and less thick than those of hawks. They make a raspy "kack-kack-kack" sound when in flight. The peregrine falcon is distinctive in that it kills its prey in the air, flying at speeds of up to 200 mph. Small birds are plucked from the air, while larger birds are knocked out in an explosion of feathers.

After taking in the scenery, we began to descend, the cold rain hitting us with full force. Because the trip is so short—.9 mile—we took our time going down the mountain to avoid the chance of a nasty fall on the steep, slippery sections.

peregrine falcon

To get there

From Route 9 in Ausable Forks turn right at the Stewart's Shop on Main Street and drive a short distance to a stop sign, then turn left onto Silver Lake Road. The trail head is approximately 10 miles from Ausable Forks and is on the right. It is marked by a yellow-on-brown DEC sign.

From the west, the parking area is one mile east of Silver Lake on the left.

Technical information
Height: 2,374'
Trail Length: .9 mile
Difficulty: Moderately easy

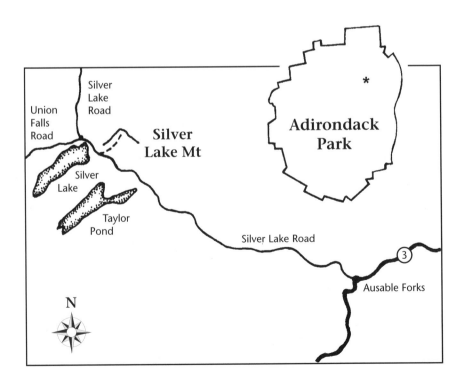

Chapter 27

Looking south from Cobble Hill with Algonquin and higher peaks in the distance.

Cobble Hill makes for a perfect winter climb on skis or snow-shoes, but the great views from atop this small nub that rises just northeast of Lake Placid Village provides enjoyable scenery at any time of year. Located just minutes from the bustling Main Street traffic of the tourist-oriented village, Cobble can be a quiet, temporary escape from the crowds.

I last climbed Cobble Hill a week before Christmas, expecting to find Currier and Ives-like views of the picturesque village and ski area below, all framed by snow-capped mountains. I wasn't disappointed.

The day I did the climb, there were eight inches of hard-packed snow on the ground, more appropriate for boots than skis, but I carried along light-weight, high-tech metal, polypropylene-decked snowshoes.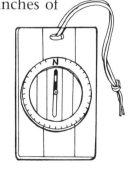

The trail head is off a private road that enters the Whitney Road just outside of town. Here I parked and walked a quarter of a mile to where the trail starts with boulders on the right and a

Trail head for Cobble Hill off private road. Though posted, hikers and cross-country skiers are allowed across property to where ascent begins.

sign that warns against hunting, trapping and fishing, but allows hikers and skiers the use of the trail.

After a short 50-yard walk, I crossed a narrow plank bridge over a small brook. From here, there is a junction with the Cobble Hill trail going left toward Echo Lake; its frozen surface was off in the distance. The hike here, through snow-covered softwoods, still is on private property, so staying on the path is essential.

At the end of Echo Lake, there is a private home on the left. The trail, marked by a weathered sign, veers right and begins to climb through a young hardwood forest.

Along this stretch there are a series of zigzagging switchbacks, obviously created with the skier in mind. In addition, the carefully logged forest had openings where I could see Wilmington Notch off in the distance to the east, Mirror Lake and Lake Placid to the northwest, and the ski jump to the west.

Finally I reached the summit and walked to the west-facing cliffs that are visible from the road.. It was here two years earlier that Northwood School students practiced mountain search and rescue techniques under the tutelage of wilderness rescue instructor Tommy Condon and Northwood Assistant Headmaster Don Mellor, who

The trail up Cobble Hill is a cross-country skier's delight, with numerous switchbacks and openings that provide great views.

is also a well-known rock climber and author. During the exercise, a hiker was lifted down the cliffs in a simulated rescue drill.

Because of its proximity to Northwood School, Cobble Hill is frequently climbed by students, so there are a variety of trails, especially in winter, emanating from the hill. Though there is access through Northwood, the most direct, least confusing route up the hill, albeit a little longer, is the way I took, and I was the only person on the summit that day.

From atop Cobble, I could see Wilmington Notch more clearly than from along the trail, as well as the Sentinel Range, and to the south Algonquin and Marcy. The village of Lake Placid, dressed up for the holidays, had a postcard look that was even more accentuated by the clouds blocking the winter sunlight.

After spending time taking in the scenery, I descended the way I came. I was tempted to take the shortcut down by the side of the cliffs, but my common sense took over—that, and not wanting to become a part of a real life mountain rescue.

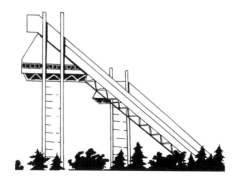

To Get There

From Route 86 just south of the Lake Placid Village, turn onto the Northwood Road (the Cobble Hill Inn is on the corner). Drive .7 mile (you will pass the Northwood School) to a stop sign. Turn right on Whitney Road 1 mile to where a private road enters on the right.

Park off the side of the road here and walk .25 mile to where you will see boulders blocking a clearing on the right. There is a sign that warns against hunting, trapping or fishing, but hikers and skiers are allowed to pass through.

Technical Information
Height: 2,343 feet
Trail Length: .9 mile
Difficulty: Moderately easy

*
Adirondack
Park

Lake
Placid

Mirror
Lake

Whitney Rd

Echo
Lake

Nothwood Rd

86

86

**Cobble
Hill**

N

Chapter 28

Panoramic view from Baker looking north.

There may be no mountain in the Adirondacks more accessible than Baker. It rises just outside the village of Saranac Lake, a community whose population of about 6,000 almost doubles during the summer months.

Although the trail head is an easy drive from most area highways, once the climb begins—if you choose the right time of year—you can quickly escape most vestiges of civilization.

In the past, I climbed Baker during the summer, when I usually met up with other hikers along the trail. Then I decided to give Baker a try in the winter. In early February, the day before the start of the popular Saranac Lake Winter Carnival, I pulled off the side of East Pine Street where a yellow-on-brown sign marks the trail. It was 8 a.m. and the temperature registered minus 8.

The trail rises gradually at first through birches and balsams. Though there hadn't been any recent snowfall, clumps of old snow still clung to some balsam limbs. Early on, there are a couple of spur routes that

Trail marker for Baker Mountain climb.

branch off to the left. Stay on the beaten path to the right; red DEC
signs mark the way.

Because of the lack of recent snow when I made my trip, the
trail showed signs of use throughout the climb; it had been com-
pressed by snowshoes, boots, dog paws and cross-country skis. In
fact, it was so compacted that no snowshoes were needed. Even so,
I carried along a pair of lightweight, metal-framed, polypropylene
decked snowshoes that had crampons attached to their bindings.
In real slippery sections, these could be worn to prevent slipping
and falling. I wore layered clothing with an inner
layer of polypropylene and an outer of fleece. Since
there was no wind on that cold, still morning, I left
the light windbreaker in my truck.

One difference between a summer and a winter
climb up Baker is the almost instant gratification—
views of the surrounding countrywide—you get in
winter after climbing but a short distance. With the
hardwoods leafless, I caught glimpses of Saranac
Lake village, Lower Saranac Lake, and surrounding
areas after a short ascent to a white ash-covered

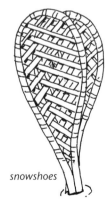

snowshoes

Baker Mountain with frozen Moody Pond in foreground.

ridge. From that vantage point, I could also see the summit of Baker in the distance and the general direction of the trail I would take to climb the mountain.

Soon the hardwoods gave way to hemlocks just before the .3 mile steep ascent to the top. On the slopes, the snow depth was only six inches, an indication both of the light snowfall and the sun's warming rays hitting the open areas. I met few obstructions and little debris on the trail.

In places along that final climb, there were very slippery sections of trail. Rather than putting on my snowshoes, I took it slowly, easing over glare ice, sometimes on my hands and knees. Finally I came out on a bare area just below the summit. The cliffs were on my right, so I proceeded forward at a snail's pace, planting each step carefully. Care must be used traversing from here to the summit.

From the top, I could easily see Saranac Lake village, Lake Flower, Lower Saranac and Middle Saranac. To the east, the sun's morning glare was just gaining strength above the mass of MacKenzie Mountain; it was too bright to take a photograph. Scotch pines of all different sizes are the most common trees near the top. They are not a native species, so I guessed they were the result of seeds from trees in nearby fields and yards that were deposited by wind and birds.

I spent a short time on the summit, then packed up and headed down. The trail down that day was difficult and I took my time, inching through the really steep, slick stretches. I usually don't stop to take photographs or make notes on the ascent of my hikes. I don't take the cameras out until I reach the top; then, on the trip down, I do my photography and note-taking of trees, trail conditions and the like.

The hike back to the trail head, even in winter, can be done in an hour or less, and, although Baker is not remote nor overly high, I found that climbing it during the cold season

Scotch pine (foreground), Lake Flower and Lower Saranac Lake in distance from above Baker Mountain cliffs.

provided a great contrast from those summer climbs, which are quite a bit easier, and the trip was a good way to escape the notorious "cabin fever" that strikes in the mountains during midwinter.

To Get There

From Route 3 on the east side of Saranac Lake village, turn off on Pine Street. After a short distance, take a sharp left on East Pine Street. The road first goes over a small bridge, then skirts Moody Pond. The trail head is near the head of the pond. There is a yellow-on-brown state trail marker that reads "Saranac Lake Wild Forest." Pull over; in winter leave room for plows. There is no formal parking area.

Technical Information
Height: 2,452'
Trail Length: .9 mile
Difficulty: Moderate

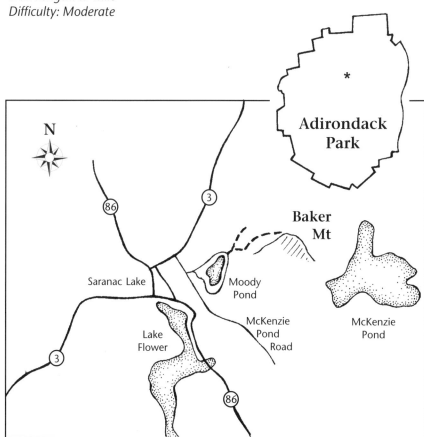

Chapter 29

Looking north just before Floodwood Mountain summit.

A hike up Floodwood Mountain, which rises deep in the heart of the St. Regis Canoe Area, is an adventure that begins on the way to the trail head. The trip to the parking area requires a 5.5-mile drive down the dirt-covered Floodwood Road and a short side road. Both are enclosed by a heavy tree canopy. This is not a good choice for a mud-season climb.

Though difficult to get to, Floodwood Mountain rewards the hiker in many ways, and for my daughter, Karalyn, and I, who hiked it in mid-June, these included great views of the Canoe Area, lots of deer signs along the way, and a major migration of large reptiles.

aspen leaf

After pulling in at the parking area, we began hiking along a sandy stretch of roadway. Here we met up with the first of the large reptiles we would see that day—a snapping turtle.

One of the female snapping turtles that cross dirt roads near Floodwood on their way to lay eggs.

In June, the female turtles leave their watery environment to search out sandy nest sites where they deposit their clutch of eggs.

Snappers are the largest turtles in northern New York, with carapaces (top shells) that measure up to 18 inches long. These turtles look even larger because of their long, thick, jagged tails, which, along with their large hooked jaws, give them a primitive look. In fact, their ancestors roamed the earth with dinosaurs.

Even though they look fierce, snappers are not aggressive unless harassed; then they lash out at their attacker. So it is a good idea, as Karalyn and I did, to give them the right of way.

In their nests, females lay two to four dozen eggs that look like ping-pong balls. Very few of the offspring, however, will survive. Predators such as foxes, skunks, and raccoons seek out turtle nests and gorge themselves on the eggs. Even though most eggs are lost, it doesn't necessarily mean the species is endangered. Females don't normally breed until they are 18 or 19 years old, and they can continue breeding until they are in their 70's. If just one or two offspring of these long-lived reptiles survive to replace the mother, the population is maintained.

We bid farewell to our turtle and continued our hike through a hardwood forest dominated by maples. Deer tracks were everywhere. After about three quarters of a mile on a tote road, where we passed a couple more snappers, we saw a sign pointing the direction for the rest of the climb. The path narrowed, but was well-marked with red DEC trail markers.

For the next half mile, we walked along fairly flat and, in places, muddy terrain, crossing a couple of brooks as we ever-so-gradually moved upward. Hardwoods like quaking aspen and poplar were the predominant trees.

Finally, the trail began to ascend, and after another half mile we reached the summit. Don't be disappointed by the modest northern views that you first see of the St. Regis Canoe Area, Floodwood Pond, and Floodwood Road; instead, climb a little farther, as we did, and follow the sign to the south face. This is a short but somewhat difficult trek because it requires some climbing up a smooth rock face. Once at this lookout, though,

Boulder-filled section of Floodwood Mountain trail.

we had great views of Iron Mountain, Wolf Pond, Tupper Lake, and even Panther Mountain to the southeast. If you are hiking with young children, you should keep a careful eye on them during this short side trip.

Once the property of the Bergen County, New Jersey Boy Scout Council, Floodwood is now open to the public, and its remote setting certainly makes the adventurous trip and climb a worthwhile venture.

To get there

Take Route 3 east from Tupper Lake village to intersection with Route 30. Take Route 30 north for about eight miles to Floodwood Road, which is on the left just before Saranac Inn. Follow Floodwood Road 6.4 miles until a sign for the Floodwood Scout Reservation appears on the left. Turn here and drive .3 mile to a well-marked public parking area. From the parking area, follow the road about .7 mile to where the marked trail begins.

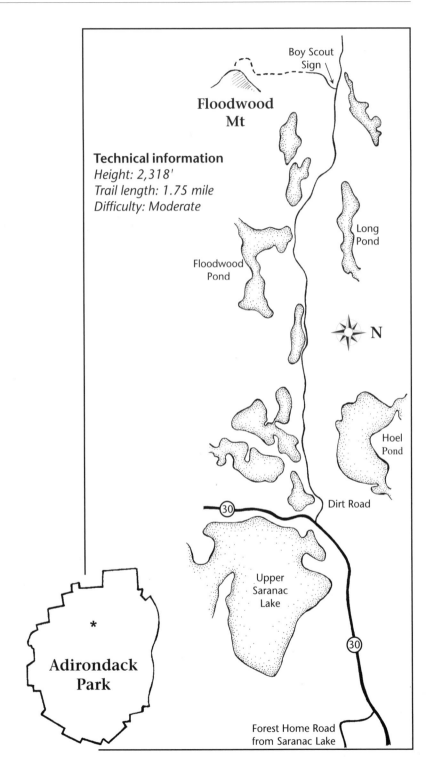

Boy Scout
Sign

**Floodwood
Mt**

Technical information
Height: 2,318'
Trail length: 1.75 mile
Difficulty: Moderate

Long
Pond

Floodwood
Pond

N

Hoel
Pond

Dirt Road

30

Upper
Saranac
Lake

30

*

**Adirondack
Park**

Forest Home Road
from Saranac Lake

Chapter 30

Karalyn Aprill surveys countryside from atop Panther Mountain.*

We sat on the bare rock outcrop, scanning the horizon. To our left was a deep blue sliver of Stony Creek Pond; below us, Follensby Pond sparkled in the sunlight; off in the distance, an expanse of Tupper Lake cut through the forest. We were alone, my daughter and I, sitting atop the very unassuming 2,237-foot Panther Mountain that rises between Tupper and Upper Saranac lakes. The peace and quiet we felt on that Memorial Day was quite a contrast to the raucous hordes of hikers who had packed into the High Peaks via the Adirondack Loj trail head 19 miles to our east. We had chosen Panther for the solitude.

Our climb started at the marked parking area opposite the trail head off busy Route 3. The cool morning air kept the blackflies at bay. Carefully, we crossed this busy thoroughfare and immediately began to ascend. The trail, covered with brown softwood spills, wove through large hemlocks.

* Do not confuse this Panther Mountain, in Franklin County, with the Panther Mountain in Chapter 14, in Hamilton County.

The panther, also called cougar or mountain lion.

As we continued upward, we encountered many wet spots, some quite slippery. White birch and other hardwoods mixed with the softwoods as the elevation increased. At .9 mile, we reached the 2,237-foot summit of Panther, an open rock mass that would have provided an excellent lookout for the peak's namesake--the panther, also called mountain lion or cougar.

These big cats, weighing from 135 to 175 pounds, were never plentiful in the Adirondacks, but roamed here as late as the end of the 19th century. There are many who believe a few big cats still wander the Adirondacks today.

In historical records such as *Adventures in the Wilderness*, by W.H.H. "Adirondack" Murray, written in 1869, there is no lack of hyperbole when it comes to these animals. Murray describes one this way: "An animal which often measures 12 feet from tip to tip and is the slyest, strongest, bloodiest ranger in the woods."

Because of their perceived threat to the deer herd, the state legislature put a $20 bounty, a considerable sum in those days, on panthers, and by 1896, records state that 99 of the animals had been turned in for bounty money. This total should not be taken as fact, however; bounty records are very inaccurate. For example, it is claimed that one hunter used the same mountain lion head to collect as many as 50 bounties!

Trail up Panther Mountain starts just off busy Route 3 west of Saranac Lake village.

By 1900, panthers were thought to be extirpated from New York State, but sightings are reported every year, so many that some DEC officials don't dismiss them as cases of mistaken identity. Still, if there really are a few panthers passing through the Adirondacks, no one knows where they come from or where they are going. The panther, a solitary creature of the big woods, is a protected species in New York State today.

In a way, my daughter and I were acting like panthers that Memorial Day, shying away from the crowds, enjoying our own private vantage to view the mountains.

When we descended an hour later on Panther's meandering, moderately steep trail, the only sound of civilization was the increasing rumble of traffic on Route 3 as we approached the parking area. We speculated that these drivers might have been in a hurry to get to a more popular nearby trail, like that up Ampersand Mountain. If so, they had overlooked one of the little treasures of the Adirondack low peaks.

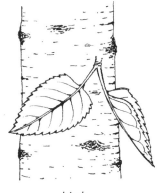

birch

To get there

From the east, take Route 3 west of Saranac Lake village about 11 miles. The parking area is just past the Cold River Ranch sign on the left.

From the west, take Route 3 east from Tupper Lake village until 1.5 miles past its intersection with Route 30.

Technical information
Height: 2,237'
Trail length: .9 mile
Difficulty: Moderate

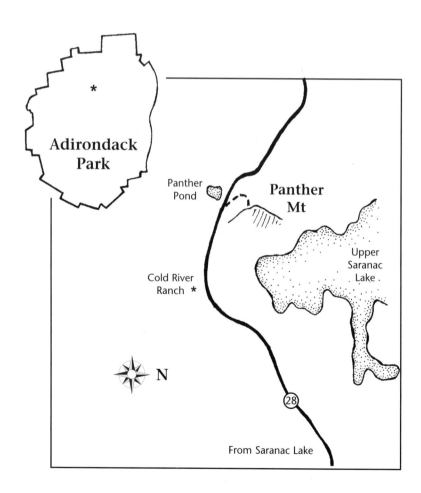

Chapter 31

From Owls Head, looking across lower section of Long Lake to mountains beyond.

I climbed Owls Head Mountain on a Wednesday after Labor Day weekend. The conditions couldn't have been better: most of the holiday crowd was gone and it was still too early for the leaf peepers. The morning was clear and cool, and by the time I reached the summit of Owls Head, the sun was illuminating a beautiful panorama of the Adirondack heartland.

The trail to Owls Head begins off Endion Road, just north of Long Lake village. I left my car in the empty parking lot early in the morning, and began to climb. At first, a number of snowmobile trails cross the Owls Head trail, which is identified first with red markers, later with white-on-orange triangles.

After one mile there is an intersection with a marker pointing left toward Owls Head. The forest here is predominantly hardwoods. The trail, mostly level, continues for a way until it meets up with a small stream. Then it rises, paralleling the stream. This section proved a little rough, requiring travel over rocks and through water and mud.

Remains of fire warden's cabin below Owls Head tower.

I finally reached a level piece of land, then descended a little to where I found the remains of a fire warden's cabin. All that was left were the stone pillars; the tower atop Owls Head has been unmanned for years. In many places in this section of the trail, clumps of honey mushrooms grew on dead stumps and roots.

After examining the cabin, I began to climb again, this time up and over ledges that were quite steep. I

honey mushrooms

grabbed for trees or anything solid to help pull myself up. Just before the summit, I approached a tunnel of vegetation--trees blown over yet suspended high enough so I could pass underneath.

Although I hadn't yet reached the summit, I could hear hawks riding the thermals, calling to one another as they soared around the top of the mountain. Then, a short way beyond the tunnels, the foliage gave way to the open summit and fire tower with fantastic views on that clear morning. To the east, I could see Blue, Kempshall, and Santanoni mountains with the High Peaks in the distance.

Intersection of trail to Owls Head, one of many that hikers encounter early in the climb.

Below was a thin band of Long Lake; the rest of the big lake was hidden by mountains. Two hawks glided a short distance in front of me, providing motion to the scene. Then a float plane, probably based in Long Lake, took off in the distance.

The fire tower, as with many that are abandoned by the DEC and unsponsored, had the lower flight of steps removed. I did not try to shimmy up to the first intact steps; the view from the summit was spectacular enough.

After taking in the scenery and eating a snack, I headed down the mountain, a trip that required some careful footing through the steep stretch down to the old cabin foundation. Along the way I met up with two college students making the climb. They were the only hikers I saw during the trip.

Owls Head is the highest of the "low peaks" and the trail to its summit is the second longest in the series. Considering the great views, accentuated by the soaring hawks, I felt the effort was well worth it.

hawk

To get there

From Long Lake village, take Route 30 north .6 miles past the bridge over Long Lake to where Endion Road enters on the left. Drive down Endion 1.5 miles to the parking area on the right.

Technical information
Height: 2,748'
Trail length: 3.1 miles
Difficulty: Moderately difficult

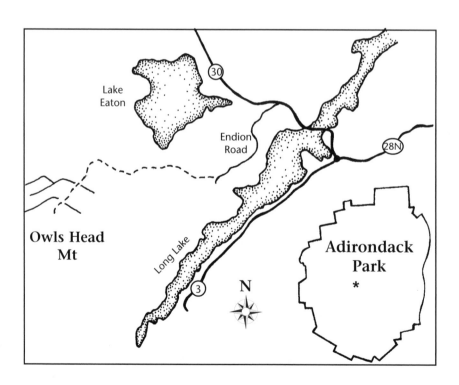

Chapter 32

Looking out from atop Goodnow; Rich Lake is in foreground.

If mountain trails were categorized like human personality types, there would be some that could only be described as cantankerous—difficult to deal with, climbing steadily upward through piles of rocks. Others could be labeled friendly and cooperative, with their smooth-surfaced, gently inclined paths.

If I had to categorize the trail up Goodnow Mountain near Newcomb in the heart of the Adirondacks, I would call it polite or genteel: it takes you up steep inclines, then eases you down on straightaways. Your ascent up the 2,685-foot peak, complete with fire tower and magnificent views, is, at times, like climbing a spiral staircase with rustic benches positioned at key points where you can sit down, relax, and admire the scenery.

The Goodnow trail is not only easy on your heart muscles, but it is stimulating to your mind. Throughout the two-mile ascent, there are numbered and lettered learning stations that explain local natural history. For example, Station C is placed before an ancient hemlock tree that is about 250 years old. A brochure, avail-

One of many benches for hikers to catch their breath on the way up Goodnow.

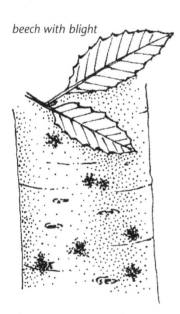

beech with blight

able at the trail head sign-in, explains more about the specifics of this tree and hemlocks in general. Other stations tell about wildlife, geology, decay, the role of pathogens on a beech forest, and man's effect on the forest.

In the middle of a week in August, I climbed Goodnow. The morning was cool and clear and mine was the only car in the parking area, 1.5 miles west of the Newcomb Adirondack Park Visitor Interpretive Center (VIC) on Route 28N.

The trail rose immediately, but the ascent wasn't long. I was soon back on level ground as I walked north toward the mountain. Throughout the trail, there are boardwalks over wet spots and bridges over small brooks.

The trail is owned and maintained by the State University of New York (SUNY) College of Environmental Science and Forestry in Newcomb. Sylvester Goodnow, the original settler of the area, homesteaded at the base of the mountain in the 1920s.

After climbing through a hardwood forest mixed with hemlocks, I came to my first lookout, a cleared piece of forest that acts as a window looking south. In the distance were Blue Mountain and the Fishing Brook Range. Farther on, past the ruins of Archer Huntington's cabin retreat (Huntington, once the owner of this land, donated his Newcomb estate to SUNY), the trail opened even more, with a final climb to the rock-covered, partially open summit.

While the views on that crisp, clear morning were impressive, it took a climb up the refurbished fire tower to observe the entire spectacle. At the top of the first flight of stairs, Rich Lake appeared below to the north; on the second flight, the Seward Range, Santanoni, Algonquin, Colden, and Marcy stood out in the distance.

By the third and fourth flights, a 360-degree panorama of the Adirondacks was visible. To the west were Windfall, Kempshall, and Big Tupper mountains; to the east and southeast, Lake Harris, Vanderwhacker, and Gore mountains. From that fire tower, as the mountain scenery unfolded in all directions, I felt that I was standing high over the heartland of the Adirondack Park.

After descending the tower and while inspecting the old tower keeper's cabin, now used by SUNY, a scarlet tanager, that bright red bird with black wings, landed on a nearby branch, adding even more color to the impressive scene.

On the way down Goodnow Mountain, I met the first of what would be five different groups of people climbing this low peak that morning. So for those wanting solitude on their climb, it is a good idea to start out early.

scarlet tanager

The descent was as easy as the climb--no major rock piles or exposed root sections to tangle with or trip you up. This was appropriate for such a polite mountain path as the Goodnow trail.

A side trip to the VIC

The Goodnow Mountain hike is most enjoyable when combined with a visit to the Adirondack Park Visitor Interpretive Center (518-582-2000) 1.5 miles east of the trail head. Here there are clean bathrooms, picnic facilities, easy-walking nature trails, and a gift shop. In addition, in September, Newcomb celebrates Teddy Roosevelt Days. The festivities include canoe and kayak races, woodsmen's demonstrations, dinners, concerts, fireworks, and children's games at the VIC.

To get there

From the south, take the Northway (I-87) to Exit 23 (Warrensburg). Go north on Route 9 to Route 28 and continue to North Creek, where Route 28N branches off to the right. The Goodnow trail head is about 25 miles from the intersections of routes 28 and 28N, 1.5 miles west of the VIC.

From the north, take Northway Exit 29 (Newcomb) and drive west on Blue Ridge. Follow 28N to trail head, 1.5 miles west of the VIC.

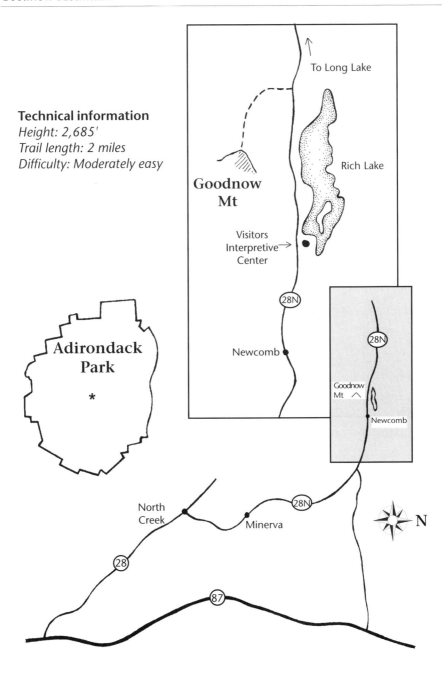

Technical information
Height: 2,685'
Trail length: 2 miles
Difficulty: Moderately easy

Chapter 33

Schroon Lake from lookout near top of Severance Hill.

Hill is a good word to describe Severance, a small knob of rock and earth rising just west of Northway Exit 28. At 1,693 feet it is hardly mountain-sized, yet as a first climb, a relaxed walk for youngsters, or a trek for older hikers, Severance Hill is a good choice. And from the two lookouts, there are some nice views of Schroon Lake and points beyond.

Getting to the trail head is as easy as the climb. Just take North-way Exit 28 and drive one half mile south on Route 9; the trail head and parking area are on the right. One day in June, I pulled over at just this spot and, with my daughter, Karalyn, began the climb.

The hike starts in an unusual manner: the trail goes through two large oblong culverts under the Northway. It felt kind of weird to be walking underneath large tractor trailers and fast-moving cars.

These culverts are similar to those ten miles to the north, where they connect two sides of the big North Hudson deer yard that was bisected when the Northway was built. To protect both the deer and drivers, fences were erected along the north and southbound

149

Severance climb starts with trip through culvert below Northway.

lanes, with the culverts designed to funnel the deer from one side to the other.

The North Hudson yard, or wintering area, is home to hundreds of deer who chew up all edible vegetation within reach. There is a browse line that looks evenly pruned. In bad winters, deer will even eat balsam and spruce, which don't provide the nutrients or the digestibility of cedar or hardwoods.

After passing through the culverts at Exit 28, we began to walk gradually upward through a forest of hemlocks and white pine, their spills cushioning the trail. Some of these trees were quite large, and they helped to muffle the Northway traffic noises as we continued to climb.

In a half hour, we came to the first lookout, an opening that revealed the expanse of Schroon Lake off in the distance with the Pharoah Lake Wilderness beyond it. A little farther on there is a second lookout that shows the more northerly part of Schroon Lake and Paradox Lake and the community of Severance. Supposedly, the settlement and hill were named for settlers who took up residence here in the early 1800s.

The climb ends at the second lookout, unless one is determined to climb farther on to the wooded summit that provides no views; it is a short distance beyond the lookout.

deer in snow

Our descent, more like an easy walk down, was uneventful, and we knew we were getting close to the trail head by the increased rumble of traffic. The entire two-mile round trip can easily be completed in an hour or two.

Suggestions for a full-day trip

Although the focus of this book has been to relax, take it easy, and enjoy the solitude and views, some people like to take full-day trips. Here's a possible scenario that will com-

One of the many large white pines that grow beside the trail up Severance.

bine nature and history: First, you can climb Severance. Then, if you want to immerse yourself in some of the area's historical events, you can travel about 18 miles on Highway 74 east to Ticonderoga and visit Fort Ticonderoga and its museum. After spending some time at the Fort, drive south a short distance and climb Cook Mountain (see Chapter 8). If you are to return south, drive along Highway 9N over the Tongue Range (Five Mile Mountain area) to Lake George village. Here you will find another museum at Fort William Henry, a restored fort that dates back to the French and Indian War. The Northway is only a short drive from the Fort.

To get there

To reach Severance Hill, take Northway Exit 28 to Route 9 and drive south one-half mile. The parking area is on the right.

Technical information
Height: 1,693'
Trail length: 1 mile
Difficulty: Easy

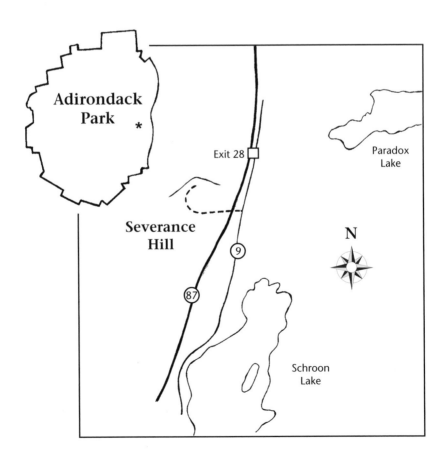

Chapter 34

View from second open area just beyond Sawyer summit.

Sawyer is another of those mountains that could jokingly be classified as a molehill, but even molehills can be interesting when they provide subtle, understated views, solitude, and clues to a major weather event in the recent past.

The marked trail head and parking area are just off heavily traveled Route 28/30 between Indian Lake and Blue Mountain Lake. Many travelers who pass by Sawyer are on their way to climb the more famous Blue Mountain or to visit the Adirondack Museum in the town of Blue Mountain Lake, and don't even glance over at the unobtrusive knob that sits 4.5 miles northwest of Indian Lake. But those who do stop and give Sawyer a try are treated to a very relaxed climb, one of the easiest in the Adirondacks.

From the trail head, the narrow path gradually rises, levels, then descends for a short way through young hardwoods. Scattered about are the remains of some much larger trees, those that were in the path of the heavy winds that pushed through the western Adirondacks on July 15, 1995.

Large trees, split in two by massive windstorm of July 1995. Sawyer Mountain was in the path of the gale.

On that summer day, during an event that has been described as 20 minutes of terror, a massive wind blew through this area in what might have been an air inversion or tornado-like storm. The result was 126,000 acres of forest disturbed, with 60 percent of the trees, including old-growth forests, demolished. The storm caused millions of dollars in damage, closed many hiking trails, and resulted in heated debate on how to clean up the mess.

In early August, 1995, I climbed Sawyer for the first time. Boles of large trees, split in two, were scattered about. The trail had been recently re-opened, but the storm's destruction still could be seen back in the woods. When I returned to Sawyer two years later, many of these trees were camouflaged by the inevitable new growth, with a new succession of forest reappearing.

After the dip, the trail rises again until a lookout opens to the left below the mountain's summit. Here the High Peaks are visible. I continued on, crossing Sawyer's wooded top to another window beyond. From this outlook, I could see Blue and Wakely mountains and unending forest stretching to the horizon.

On my return, even while taking it easy, I was back to the car in a little over half an hour. For those interested in winter snowshoe climbs, Sawyer is certainly one to consider. It is a small mountain that requires little effort to ascend, yet the path to the summit has a lot to offer, if only for insights into the great windstorm of 1995.

To get there

Take Route 28/30 4.5 miles northwest of Indian Lake village. The parking area and DEC yellow-on-brown sign at the trail head are on the left.

Technical information
Height: 2,500'
Trail length: 1.1 miles
Difficulty: Easy

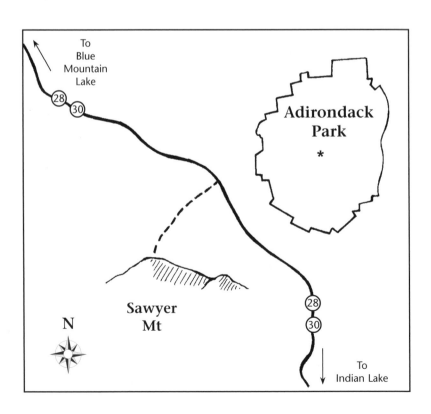

Chapter 35

Looking west from the top of Chimney Mountain.

Chimney is an uncommon mountain. People climb it not only for its great views, but for its unusual rock formations, which geologists believe were made by cataclysmic events in the past.

On a Tuesday in August, my daughter, Karalyn, and I climbed the 2,500-foot peak that lies due east of Indian Lake to explore some of Chimney's secrets.

The trail head and parking area are owned by the Chimney Mountain Wilderness Lodge. Since this is private property, there is a $1.00 parking fee. After crossing a field, we began to ascend the mountain, gradually at first through a typical Adirondack hardwood forest of maples, beech, and both yellow and white birch.

157

Spider web on the trail.

It was 9 a.m.; I knew we would be the first up the mountain that day because the long strands of spider webs connected to bushes along the way were undisturbed. We would have the mountain to ourselves, if only for a short time.

About halfway or one-half mile up the mountain the grade gets steeper, becoming very steep near the summit. Just before the top there is a trail on the left that follows a rift valley below the summit. For those interested in caves and natural crevices, this is the trail to take.

There are many stories surrounding the making of these caves, some of which go down 50 feet or more. Most geologists think the rift was created by geological activity thousands of years ago—a short time by rock-forma-tion standards. As a result, in some sections huge boulders are strewn about the path and can be very difficult to maneuver around.

But it was the unusual formation on the top of

The larger chimney.

the mountain that attracted us this time, so Karalyn and I took the main trail on the right to the summit.

At first, as we neared the top, we caught glimpses of Bullhead and Puffer mountains to the east and southeast. As we walked farther west, the first, smaller chimney, a column of rock, appeared from behind the vegetation, but this was only a teaser. A little farther on, we came to the main chimney, a 35-foot mass of rock that stood out starkly against the sky. In the shadow of this massive pillar, we climbed on one of the many scattered boulders, which made a great vantage

One of the many unusual rock formations atop Chimney Mountain.

point for viewing Kings Flow and the trail head in the foreground, with Baldface Mountain, the Blue Ridge Wilderness, and Blue Mountain off in the distance.

As we moved about the summit, we found small cave-like crevices, boulders balanced precariously, and some odd-shaped stones. We spent an hour exploring the rest of the mountaintop. When it came time to leave, our choices were to backtrack or take what appeared to be another, rougher trail that looped down into the valley, passing the caves. We chose to backtrack, leaving the loop for another day. *Extreme care should be taken in the caves and only experienced rock climbers should try to ascend the tall chimney.*

On our descent, we met up with the first of the many groups of people that were starting up the mountain—81 hikers in all. They ranged in age from about three years old to a couple in their 70's. Some of the younger climbers carried ropes and pitons, obviously anticipating a day of cave exploring or climbing the chimney structure itself. But whatever activities these hikers had planned, I was sure they would be as impressed by Chimney's wonders as I had been earlier that day.

To get there

From the south, take the Northway to Warrensburg Exit 23, then Route 9 north to the Route 28 cutoff. Take Route 28 north through Wevertown and North Creek to just after the "Welcome to Indian Lake Village" sign. Look for Parkerville Road on the left. Drive down this dirt road until it meets up with Big Brook Road, roughly four miles. Turn left and stay on Big Brook Road until you pass a private property sign, then come out at the parking area and trail head.

Technical information
Height: 2,500'
Trail length: 1 miles
Difficulty: Moderate

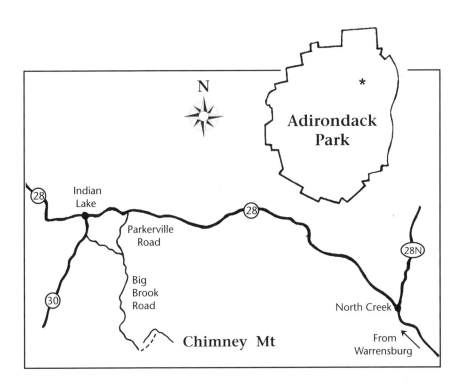

Poke-O-Moonshine Mountain

Date: _____

Climbing Partners: _____

_____

Weather: _____

Trip Highlights:

_____

_____

_____

_____

_____

_____

_____

_____

_____

_____

_____

_____

_____

_____

_____

_____

_____

_____

Coon Mountain

Date: _____

Climbing Partners: _____

_____

Weather: _____

Trip Highlights:

_____

_____

_____

_____

_____

_____

_____

_____

_____

_____

_____

_____

_____

_____

_____

_____

_____

_____

_____

_____

_____

Baxter Mountain

Date:—————————————

Climbing Partners: —————————————————————————

—————————————————————————

Weather: —————————————————————————

Trip Highlights:

—————————————————————————
—————————————————————————
—————————————————————————
—————————————————————————
—————————————————————————
—————————————————————————
—————————————————————————
—————————————————————————
—————————————————————————
—————————————————————————
—————————————————————————
—————————————————————————
—————————————————————————
—————————————————————————
—————————————————————————
—————————————————————————
—————————————————————————
—————————————————————————
—————————————————————————

Belfry Mountain

Date:————————————

Climbing Partners: ——————————————————

———————————————————

Weather: ————————————————————

Trip Highlights:

————————————————————
————————————————————
————————————————————
————————————————————
————————————————————
————————————————————
————————————————————
————————————————————
————————————————————
————————————————————
————————————————————
————————————————————
————————————————————
————————————————————
————————————————————
————————————————————
————————————————————
————————————————————
————————————————————

Cook Mountain

Date: _____

Climbing Partners: _____

_____

Weather: _____

Trip Highlights:

_____

_____

_____

_____

_____

_____

_____

_____

_____

_____

_____

_____

_____

_____

_____

_____

_____

_____

_____

_____

Treadway Mountain

Date: _____

Climbing Partners: _____

_____

Weather: _____

Trip Highlights:

_____
_____
_____
_____
_____
_____
_____
_____
_____
_____
_____
_____
_____
_____
_____
_____
_____
_____
_____
_____

five Mile Mountain

Date: _____

Climbing Partners: _____
_____

Weather: _____

Trip Highlights:

_____
_____
_____
_____
_____
_____
_____
_____
_____
_____
_____
_____
_____
_____
_____
_____
_____
_____
_____
_____

Buck Mountain

Date: _____

Climbing Partners: _____

_____

Weather: _____

Trip Highlights:

_____

_____

_____

_____

_____

_____

_____

_____

_____

_____

_____

_____

_____

_____

_____

_____

_____

_____

_____

_____

Hadley Mountain

Date: _____

Climbing Partners: _____
_____

Weather: _____

Trip Highlights:

_____
_____
_____
_____
_____
_____
_____
_____
_____
_____
_____
_____
_____
_____
_____
_____
_____
_____
_____

Cathead Mountain

Date: _____

Climbing Partners: _____

_____

Weather: _____

Trip Highlights:

_____
_____
_____
_____
_____
_____
_____
_____
_____
_____
_____
_____
_____
_____
_____
_____
_____
_____
_____
_____

Kane Mountain

Date:_____

Climbing Partners: _____

_____

Weather: _____

Trip Highlights:

_____

_____

_____

_____

_____

_____

_____

_____

_____

_____

_____

_____

_____

_____

_____

_____

_____

_____

_____

Good Luck Mountain

Date: _____

Climbing Partners: _____

_____

Weather: _____

Trip Highlights:

_____

_____

_____

_____

_____

_____

_____

_____

_____

_____

_____

_____

_____

_____

_____

_____

_____

_____

Echo Cliffs of Panther Mountain

Date: _____

Climbing Partners: _____
_____

Weather: _____

Trip Highlights:

_____
_____
_____
_____
_____
_____
_____
_____
_____
_____
_____
_____
_____
_____
_____
_____
_____
_____
_____
_____

Bald Mountain

Date: _____

Climbing Partners: _____

_____

Weather: _____

Trip Highlights:

_____

_____

_____

_____

_____

_____

_____

_____

_____

_____

_____

_____

_____

_____

_____

_____

_____

_____

_____

Black Bear Mountain

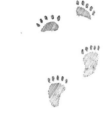

Date:—————————————

Climbing Partners: ————————————————————

————————————————————

Weather: ————————————————————

Trip Highlights:

————————————————————
————————————————————
————————————————————
————————————————————
————————————————————
————————————————————
————————————————————
————————————————————
————————————————————
————————————————————
————————————————————
————————————————————
————————————————————
————————————————————
————————————————————
————————————————————
————————————————————
————————————————————

Bear Mountain

Date: _____

Climbing Partners: _____

_____

Weather: _____

Trip Highlights:

_____

_____

_____

_____

_____

_____

_____

_____

_____

_____

_____

_____

_____

_____

_____

_____

_____

_____

_____

_____

_____

Mount Frederika

Date: _____

Climbing Partners: _____

_____

Weather: _____

Trip Highlights:

_____

_____

_____

_____

_____

_____

_____

_____

_____

_____

_____

_____

_____

_____

_____

_____

_____

_____

_____

Mount Arab

Date: _____

Climbing Partners: _____

_____

Weather: _____

Trip Highlights:

_____

_____

_____

_____

_____

_____

_____

_____

_____

_____

_____

_____

_____

_____

_____

_____

_____

_____

_____

_____

Azure Mountain

Date:————————————

Climbing Partners: ————————————————
————————————————

Weather:————————————————

Trip Highlights:

————————————————————
————————————————————
————————————————————
————————————————————
————————————————————
————————————————————
————————————————————
————————————————————
————————————————————
————————————————————
————————————————————
————————————————————
————————————————————
————————————————————
————————————————————
————————————————————
————————————————————
————————————————————
————————————————————

Jenkins Mountain

Date:————————————

Climbing Partners: ——————————————————

——————————————————————

Weather:————————————————————

Trip Highlights:

————————————————————————
————————————————————————
————————————————————————
————————————————————————
————————————————————————
————————————————————————
————————————————————————
————————————————————————
————————————————————————
————————————————————————
————————————————————————
————————————————————————
————————————————————————
————————————————————————
————————————————————————
————————————————————————
————————————————————————
————————————————————————
————————————————————————
————————————————————————

Silver Lake Mountain

Date: _____

Climbing Partners: _____

_____

Weather: _____

Trip Highlights:

_____

_____

_____

_____

_____

_____

_____

_____

_____

_____

_____

_____

_____

_____

_____

_____

_____

_____

_____

_____

Cobble Hill

Date: _____

Climbing Partners: _____

_____

Weather: _____

Trip Highlights:

_____
_____
_____
_____
_____
_____
_____
_____
_____
_____
_____
_____
_____
_____
_____
_____
_____
_____
_____
_____

Baker Mountain

Date:————————————

Climbing Partners: ————————————————

————————————————

Weather: ————————————————————

Trip Highlights:

————————————————————————

————————————————————————

————————————————————————

————————————————————————

————————————————————————

————————————————————————

————————————————————————

————————————————————————

————————————————————————

————————————————————————

————————————————————————

————————————————————————

————————————————————————

————————————————————————

————————————————————————

————————————————————————

————————————————————————

floodwood Mountain

Date: _____

Climbing Partners: _____

_____

Weather: _____

Trip Highlights:

_____

_____

_____

_____

_____

_____

_____

_____

_____

_____

_____

_____

_____

_____

_____

_____

_____

_____

_____

Panther Mountain

Date: _____

Climbing Partners: _____

_____

Weather: _____

Trip Highlights:

_____

_____

_____

_____

_____

_____

_____

_____

_____

_____

_____

_____

_____

_____

_____

_____

_____

_____

_____

Owls Head Mountain

Date: _____

Climbing Partners: _____

_____

Weather: _____

Trip Highlights:

_____

_____

_____

_____

_____

_____

_____

_____

_____

_____

_____

_____

_____

_____

_____

_____

_____

_____

_____

_____

Goodnow Mountain

Date:————————————

Climbing Partners: ————————————————————

————————————————————

Weather:————————————————————————

Trip Highlights:

————————————————————————————

————————————————————————————

————————————————————————————

————————————————————————————

————————————————————————————

————————————————————————————

————————————————————————————

————————————————————————————

————————————————————————————

————————————————————————————

————————————————————————————

————————————————————————————

————————————————————————————

————————————————————————————

————————————————————————————

————————————————————————————

————————————————————————————

Severance Mountain

Date: _____

Climbing Partners: _____
_____

Weather: _____

Trip Highlights:

_____
_____
_____
_____
_____
_____
_____
_____
_____
_____
_____
_____
_____
_____
_____
_____
_____
_____

Sawyer Mountain

Date:_____

Climbing Partners: _____

_____

Weather: _____

Trip Highlights:

_____
_____
_____
_____
_____
_____
_____
_____
_____
_____
_____
_____
_____
_____
_____
_____
_____
_____
_____
_____

Chimney Mountain

Date: _____

Climbing Partners: _____

_____

Weather: _____

Trip Highlights:

_____

_____

_____

_____

_____

_____

_____

_____

_____

_____

_____

_____

_____

_____

_____

_____

_____

_____

Technical Information

Mountain Heights (in feet)

1. Owls Head (Hamilton) 2,745
2. Hadley (|Saratoga) 2,700
3. Goodnow (Essex) 2,685
4. Mt. Arab (St. Lawrence) 2,545
5. Azure (Franklin) 2,518
6. Jenkins (Franklin) 2,514
7. Chimney (Hamilton) 2,500
8. Sawyer (Hamilton) 2,500
9. Baker (Essex) 2,452
10. Black Bear Hamilton) 2,448
11. Baxter (Essex) 2,440
12. Cathead (Hamilton) 2,423
13. Echo Cliffs/Panther Mt.* (Hamilton) 2,420
14. Silver Lake Clinton) 2,374
15. Bald (Herkimer) 2,350
16. Cobble Hill (Essex) 2,343
17. Buck (Washington) 2,334
18. Floodwood (Franklin) 2,318
19. Good Luck (Hamilton) 2,300
20. Five Mile (Warren) 2,256
21. Treadway (Essex) 2,248
22. Panther* (Franklin) 2,237
23. Frederika (Franklin) 2,200
24. Kane (Fulton) 2,200
25. Poke-O-Moonshine (Essex) 2,162
26. Bear (St. Lawrence) 2,160
27. Belfry (Essex) 1,820
28. Severance Hill (Essex) 1,693
29. Cook (Essex) 1,200
30. Coon (Essex) 1,000

Average height of all mountains is 2,271 feet

* *Note that there are two Panther Mountains, one in Franklin and one in Hamilton County.*

Mountains by County

For Further Reading

The Adirondack Book - A Complete Guide, Elizabeth Folwell, Berkshire House Publications; Lee, Massachusetts 01238

Adirondack Great Walks and Day Hikes, free from Adirondack Regional Tourism Council, PO Box 51, West Chazy, NY 12992

Adirondack Life Magazine, Jay, NY 12941

Adirondack Mountain Club Travel Guides, Adirondack Mountain Club Publications, 814 Goggins Road, Lake George, NY 12845

Adirondack Nature Guide, Sheri Amsel, Pinto Press, Mt. Kisco, NY 10549

The Adirondack Wildguide—A Natural History of the Adirondack Park, Michael G. DiNunzio; available from Adirondack Mountain Club, 814 Goggins Road, Lake George, NY 12845

Discover the Adirondacks series, Barbara McMartin, Lake View Press, distributed by North Country Books, Utica, NY 13501

North Country Books series of field guides on wild flowers, mammals, plants, trees, mushrooms and birds of the Adirondacks, North Country Books, Utica, NY 13501

About the Author

Dennis Aprill lives with his wife and two children in a remote section of the Adirondacks. A New York licensed guide (#1474), he specializes in taking individuals and groups on paths less traveled in the Adirondacks and beyond. He also teaches English and journalism classes at SUNY, Plattsburgh. He has won numerous writing and photography awards from the Outdoor Writers Association and the Outdoor Writers of Canada.

His writing includes two books: *Good Fishing in the Adirondacks* and *Mammals of the Adirondacks,* of which he was co-author. A frequent contributor to *Adirondack Life,* he is also the Outdoor Columnist for the Plattsburgh *Press-Republican*